A Quilting Life
Home & Hearth

QUILTS AND MORE TO COZY UP YOUR DECOR

Sherri L. McConnell

A Quilting Life
Home & Hearth: Quilts and More to Cozy Up Your Decor

Martingale®
18939 120th Ave NE, Suite 101
Bothell, WA 98011-9511 USA
ShopMartingale.com

Printed in Hong Kong
26 25 24 23 22 21 8 7 6 5 4 3 2 1

Library of Congress Cataloging-in-Publication Data is available upon request.

ISBN: 978-1-68356-149-1

MISSION STATEMENT

We empower makers who use fabric and yarn to make life more enjoyable.

CREDITS

PUBLISHER AND CHIEF VISIONARY OFFICER
Jennifer Erbe Keltner

CONTENT DIRECTOR
Karen Costello Soltys

TECHNICAL EDITOR
Nancy Mahoney

COPY EDITOR
Sheila Chapman Ryan

ILLUSTRATOR
Sandy Loi

DESIGN MANAGER
Adrienne Smitke

PRODUCTION MANAGER
Regina Girard

PHOTOGRAPHER
Brent Kane

SPECIAL THANKS
Some of the photography for this book was taken at Lori Clark's the FarmHouse Cottage in Snohomish, Washington.

Contents

I never thought I'd be a quilter. Even though my first endeavor with a sewing machine at the age of 10 was a patchwork pillow, that project served as an introduction to sewing a straight seam so that I could move on to making clothes (which was my passion as a tween and teenager). During my junior high and high school years, my grandmother became an avid quilter, and while I appreciated her work, I was determined not to be a quilter myself. Quilting seemed like something for older women. I couldn't understand spending so much time cutting fabrics into small pieces just to sew them back together again—until one day as a young mom I realized that making small projects and quilts would be an economical way to decorate our home. I was also inspired by a high school friend who, a few years after graduation, told me of her goal to make the majority of the decor in her home by hand.

So, I began making mini quilts, table toppers, and table runners, and as I look back now, it was my grandmother who encouraged my handicrafts. She often gave family members gifts of sets of place mats, table toppers, table runners, and pillows—that way she could make something by hand for every member of the family each Christmas. As my children got older there was also the need for me to make larger quilts for their beds, but I continued to make smaller projects to decorate our home and to give as gifts. Not only do small projects provide a quick finish, but they also allow quilters to use a variety of fabrics and have fun with different decor options. And they let us practice a variety of quilting techniques without the fear of "messing up" on a larger project.

Readers of my blog often ask me for suggestions in using quilts to decorate. In the section "Decorating with Quilts, Pillows, and Runners" (page 78), I'm hopeful that you'll find ideas for using your quilts and smaller projects to create the home you love. I'm sharing my ideas on intentional home decor and hope you'll find the storage and decorating ideas useful in your own spaces.

I also hope that you'll enjoy giving many of the projects made from this book as gifts. I've included primarily simple to intermediate projects that will be fun and fast to sew. You'll also find fun treats for quilters and sewists—a small project bag (page 63), a rotary-cutter case (page 69), and a sweet needle keeper (page 71). Make at least one of each for yourself and for your sewing friends.

~ Sherri

Dance Party

PIECED BY SHERRI McCONNELL; QUILTED BY MARION BOTT

When I was a young girl, I watched* The Brady Bunch *every day after school. I remember fondly the clothing styles on the show and the real-life lessons I learned from the episodes. How I wish I could see the reaction of my 10-year-old self if someone had told me that one day, I would make a quilt using fabric designed by Marcia Brady (Maureen McCormick) mixed with fabrics by my daughter and me. I was delighted when the yellow floral from our Happy Days collection worked beautifully as the outer border for this quilt, which was made with Maureen's Blooming Bunch collection.

FINISHED QUILT: 56" × 67½"
FINISHED BLOCK: 10" × 10"

Materials

Yardage is based on 42"-wide fabric. Fat eighths measure 9" × 21".

* 20 fat eighths of assorted prints for blocks
* 2⅜ yards of white solid for blocks, sashing, and inner border
* ⅛ yard of yellow print for sashing squares
* ⅞ yard of yellow floral for outer border
* ½ yard of green print for binding
* 3½ yards of fabric for backing
* 62" × 74" piece of batting

Cutting

All measurements include ¼"-wide seam allowances.

From *each* of the assorted prints, cut:

2 squares, 5" × 5" (40 total)
1 strip, 2½" × 21"; crosscut into:
  1 strip, 2½" × 10½" (20 total)
  1 square, 2½" × 2½" (20 total)

Continued on page 9

FABRIC SELECTION

I had a lot of fun combining fabrics for this quilt. You need only two prints for each block along with the white background. However, you could also change it up a bit and use a third print for the center square. Either way, it helps to decide on your fabric combinations before making the blocks so you can make sure you like each fabric pairing.

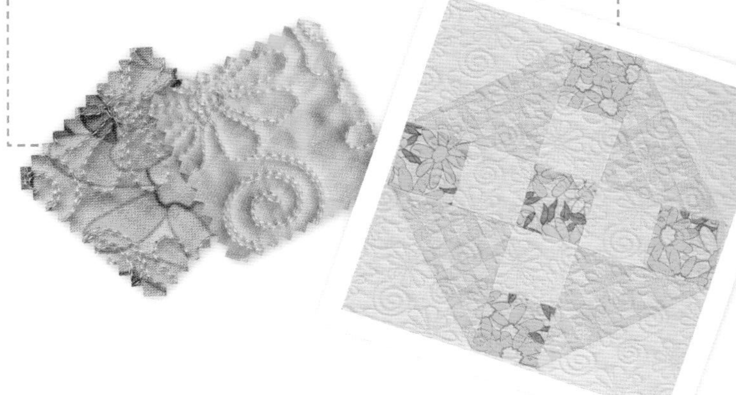

Continued from page 7

From the white solid cut:

6 strips, 5" × 42"; crosscut into 40 squares, 5" × 5"
5 strips, 2½" × 42"
17 strips, 2" × 42"; crosscut *11 of the strips* into
31 strips, 2" × 10½"

From the yellow print, cut:

12 squares, 2" × 2"

From the yellow floral, cut:

6 strips, 4½" × 42"

From the green print, cut:

7 strips, 2¼" × 42"

Making the Blocks

Press seam allowances in the directions indicated by the arrows.

1. Sew four different print 2½" × 10½" strips to the long side of a white 2½" × 42" strip to make a strip set. Make five strip sets. From each strip set, cut four sets of four matching 2½" × 4½" segments, for a total of 20 sets of four matching segments.

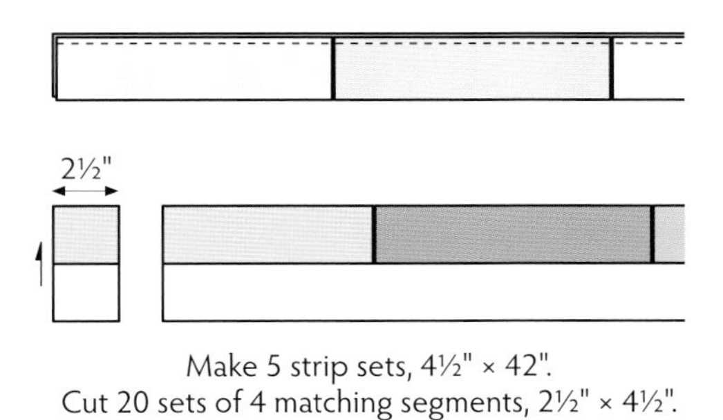

Make 5 strip sets, 4½" × 42".
Cut 20 sets of 4 matching segments, 2½" × 4½".

2. Draw a diagonal line from corner to corner on the wrong side of the white 5" squares. Layer a marked square on a print 5" square, right sides together. Sew ¼" from both sides of the drawn line; cut apart on the marked line to make two half-square-triangle units. Trim the units to measure 4½" square. Make 20 sets of four matching units.

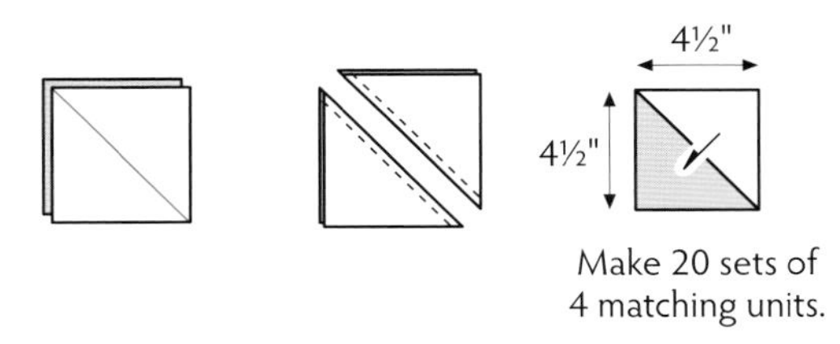

Make 20 sets of
4 matching units.

3. Lay out four matching half-square-triangle units, four matching segments from step 1, and one print 2½" square in three rows. The print in the segments and 2½" square should be the same. Sew the units, segments, and square into rows. Join the rows to make a block. Make 20 blocks measuring 10½" square, including seam allowances.

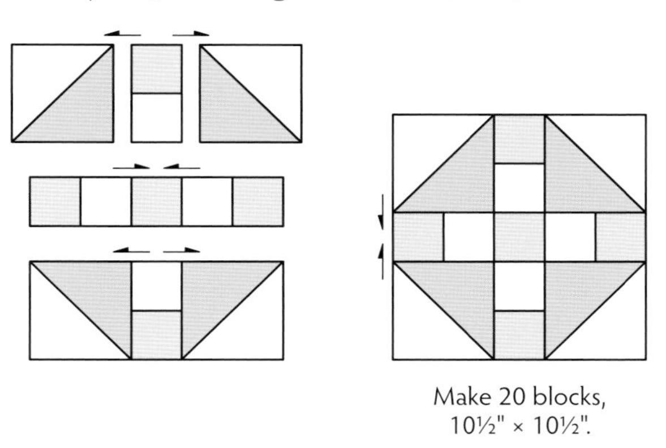

Make 20 blocks,
10½" × 10½".

Assembling the Quilt Top

1. Join four blocks and three white 2" × 10½" strips to make a block row. Make five rows measuring 10½" × 45", including seam allowances.

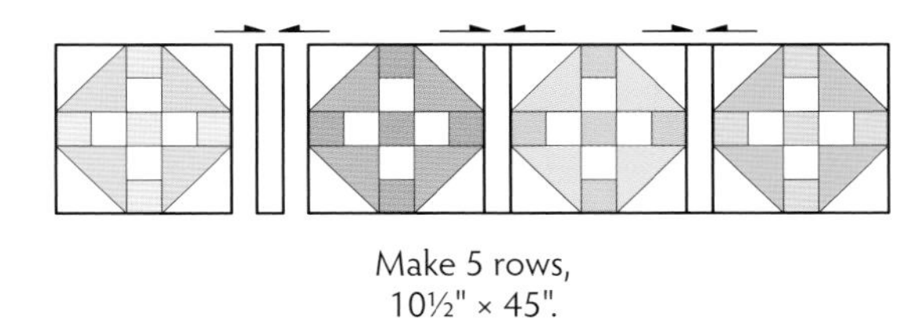

Make 5 rows,
10½" × 45".

2. Join four white 2" × 10½" strips and three yellow squares to make a sashing row. Make four rows measuring 2" × 45", including seam allowances.

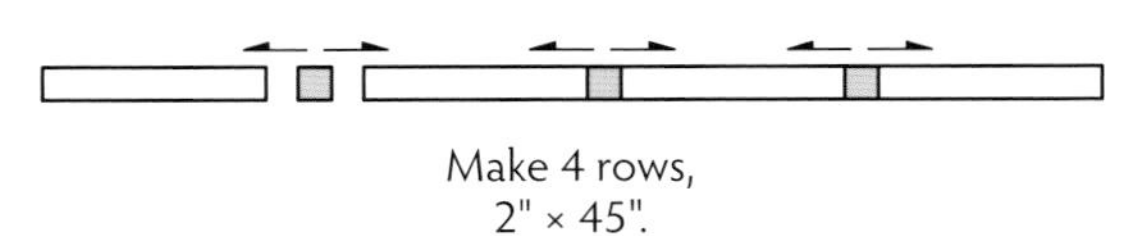

Make 4 rows,
2" × 45".

3. Join the block rows alternately with the sashing rows as shown in the quilt assembly diagram on page 10. The quilt-top center should measure 45" × 56½", including seam allowances.

4. Join the remaining white 2"-wide strips end to end. From the pieced strip, cut two 56½"-long strips

and two 48"-long strips. Sew the longer strips to opposite sides of the quilt top. Sew the shorter strips to the top and bottom edges. The quilt-top center should measure 48" × 59½", including seam allowances.

5. Join the yellow 4½"-wide strips end to end. From the pieced strip, cut two 59½"-long strips and two 56"-long strips. Sew the longer strips to opposite sides of the quilt top. Sew the shorter strips to the top and bottom edges. The quilt-top center should measure 56" × 67½".

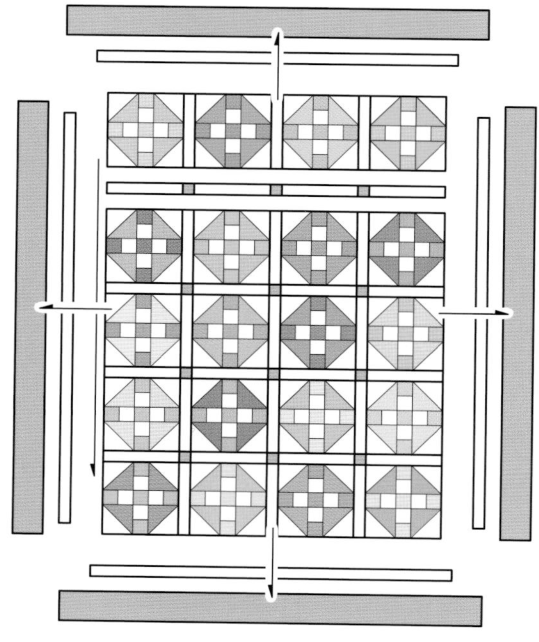

Quilt assembly

Finishing the Quilt

For more details on any finishing steps, visit ShopMartingale.com/HowtoQuilt for free downloadable information.

1. Layer the quilt top with batting and backing; baste the layers together.

2. Quilt by hand or machine. The quilt shown is machine quilted with an allover pattern of swirls and flowers.

3. Use the green 2¼"-wide strips to make binding and then attach the binding to the quilt.

Simple Patchwork Runner

PIECED BY SHERRI McCONNELL; QUILTED BY MARION BOTT

This simple but stunning runner goes together quickly and makes a big impact. It's perfect for leftover charm squares or scraps. I used fabrics from the At Home collection by Bonnie & Camille for Moda Fabrics and Happy Days collection by Sherri & Chelsi for Moda Fabrics.

FINISHED RUNNER: 16½" × 60½"
FINISHED BLOCK: 10" × 10"

Materials

Yardage is based on 42"-wide fabric.

* 21 squares, 5" × 5" *each*, of assorted prints for blocks
* ½ yard of cream print for blocks, sashing, and inner border
* ⅜ yard of navy floral for outer border
* ⅜ yard of navy print for binding
* 1⅞ yards of fabric for backing
* 23" × 67" piece of batting

Cutting

All measurements include ¼"-wide seam allowances.

From *1* of the assorted print squares, cut:
5 squares, 1½" × 1½"

From the cream print, cut:
8 strips, 1½" × 42"; crosscut *5 of the strips* into:
  6 strips, 1½" × 10½"
  20 strips, 1½" × 5"

From the navy floral, cut:
4 strips, 2½" × 42"; crosscut *1 of the strips* into
  2 strips, 2½" × 12½"

From the navy print, cut:
5 strips, 2¼" × 42"

USE YOUR SCRAPS

This block is easily adaptable for pillows, baby quilts, and even throw quilts. Keep your leftover 5" charm squares in a box so you always have a ready supply for making this block.

Making the Blocks

Press seam allowances in the directions indicated by the arrows.

Lay out four print 5" squares, four cream 1½" × 5" strips, and one print 1½" square in three rows. Sew the pieces into rows. Join the rows to make a block. Make five blocks measuring 10½" square, including seam allowances.

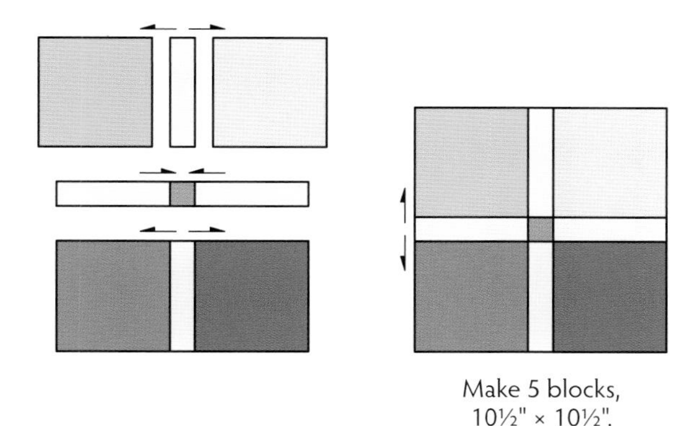

Make 5 blocks, 10½" × 10½".

Assembling the Runner

1. Lay out the blocks and cream 1½" × 10½" strips in a row, alternating them as shown in the runner assembly diagram below. Join the blocks and strips to make a row measuring 10½" × 56½", including seam allowances.

2. Join the remaining cream 1½"-wide strips end to end. From the pieced strip, cut two 56½"-long strips and sew them to the long sides of the runner top. The runner should measure 12½" × 56½", including seam allowances.

3. Sew a navy floral 2½" × 12½" strip to each short end of the runner. Join the remaining 2½"-wide strips end to end. From the pieced strip, cut two 60½"-long strips and sew them to the long sides of the runner. The runner should measure 16½" × 60½".

Finishing the Runner

For more details on any finishing steps, visit ShopMartingale.com/HowtoQuilt for free downloadable information.

1. Layer the runner top with batting and backing; baste the layers together.

2. Quilt by hand or machine. The runner shown is machine quilted with an allover diagonal grid.

3. Use the navy print 2¼"-wide strips to make binding and then attach the binding to the runner.

DRESS IT UP

You can use this easy runner to dress up different areas of your home. Measure locations where you might want to use this design, and add or subtract blocks as needed for the proper fit. Or, consider layering the runner with a longer length of linen beneath it as shown (page 12). Use holiday prints to make a runner for every season, and be sure to make some in your favorite nonseasonal decor prints.

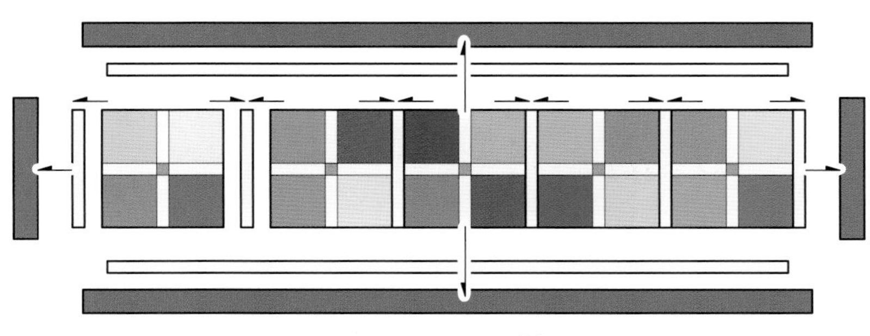

Runner assembly

Eclairs

PIECED BY SHERRI McCONNELL; QUILTED BY MARION BOTT

While this quilt is simple enough for a beginner's first project, it's also ideal for an intermediate or advanced quilter looking for a fast and fun project. Using charm squares and Jelly Roll strips for many of the block pieces also makes assembly go quickly. Be sure to choose a contrasting light fabric that will add a touch of sparkle to the quilt. I used fabrics from our Balboa collection for this quilt and love the sparkle the low-volume sun print adds as contrast.

FINISHED QUILT: 72½" × 72½"
FINISHED BLOCK: 12" × 12"

Materials

Yardage is based on 42"-wide fabric.

* 25 squares, 5" × 5" *each,* of assorted prints for blocks*
* 38 strips, 2½" × 42" *each,* of assorted dark prints for blocks*
* 1½ yards of light print for blocks and inner border
* 1¼ yards of aqua print for outer border
* ⅝ yard of coral print for binding
* 4½ yards of fabric for backing
* 79" × 79" square of batting

**I used one pack of charm squares and one Jelly Roll.*

Cutting

All measurements include ¼"-wide seam allowances. Cut the group of 13 dark strips carefully; you won't have any leftover fabric. As you cut the dark strips, keep like fabrics together.

From *each* of the assorted print squares, cut:
1 square, 4½" × 4½" (25 total)

From *each* of 25 assorted dark strips, cut:
2 strips, 2½" × 8½" (50 total)
2 strips, 2½" × 4½" (50 total)

From *each* of 13 assorted dark strips, cut:
2 strips, 2½" × 12½" (26 total)
2 strips, 2½" × 8½" (26 total)

From the light print, cut:
14 strips, 2½" × 42"; crosscut into:
  24 strips, 2½" × 12½"
  24 strips, 2½" × 8½"
7 strips, 2" × 42"

From the aqua print, cut:
8 strips, 5" × 42"

From the coral print, cut:
8 strips, 2¼" × 42"

Making the Blocks

Press seam allowances in the directions indicated by the arrows.

1. Sew matching dark 2½" × 4½" strips to opposite sides of a contrasting print 4½" square. Sew matching dark 2½" × 8½" strips to the top and bottom edges to make a center unit. The print

should be the same in all of the strips. Make 25 center units measuring 8½" square, including seam allowances.

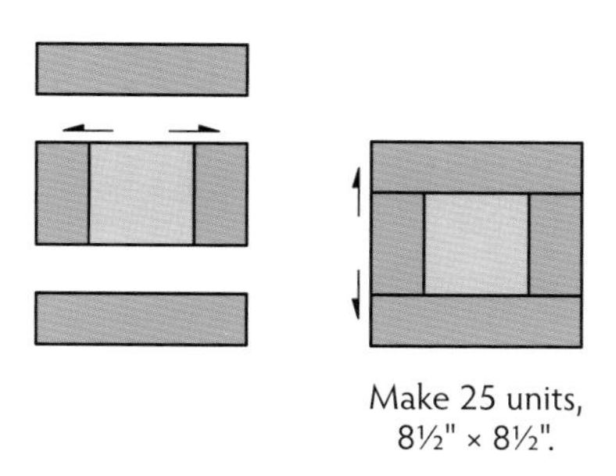

Make 25 units, 8½" × 8½".

2. Using a different dark print, sew matching dark 2½" × 8½" strips to opposite sides of a center unit. Sew matching dark 2½" × 12½" strips to the top and bottom edges to make a dark block. The dark print should be the same in all of the newly added strips. Make 13 dark blocks measuring 12½" square, including seam allowances.

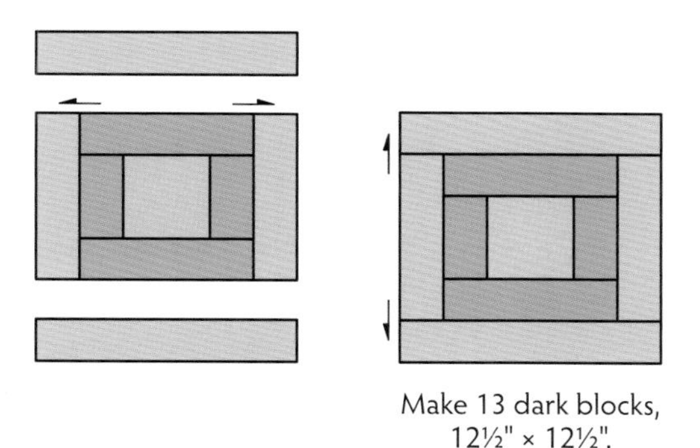

Make 13 dark blocks, 12½" × 12½".

3. Sew light 2½" × 8½" strips to opposite sides of a center unit. Sew light 2½" × 12½" strips to the top and bottom edges to make a light block. Make 12 light blocks measuring 12½" square, including seam allowances.

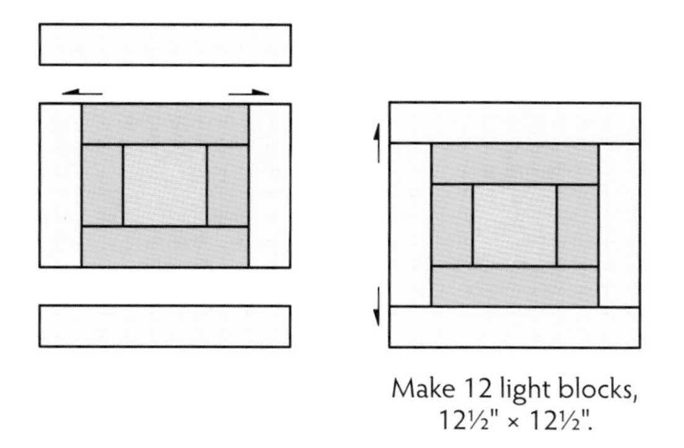

Make 12 light blocks, 12½" × 12½".

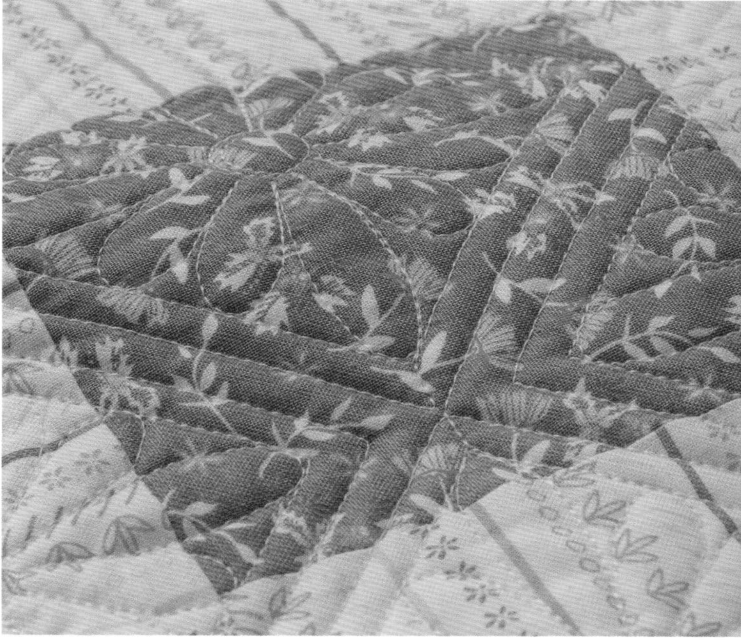

Assembling the Quilt Top

1. Lay out the dark and light blocks in five rows of five blocks each, alternating them as shown in the quilt assembly diagram below. Rotate the light blocks 90° to avoid having to match seam intersections. Sew the blocks into rows. Join the rows to make a quilt-top center measuring 60½" square, including seam allowances.

2. Join the light 2"-wide strips end to end. From the pieced strip, cut two 60½"-long strips and two 63½"-long strips. Sew the shorter strips to opposite sides of the quilt center. Sew the longer strips to the top and bottom edges. The quilt top should measure 63½" square, including seam allowances.

3. Join the aqua strips end to end. From the pieced strip, cut two 63½"-long strips and two 72½"-long strips. Sew the shorter strips to opposite sides of the quilt center. Sew the longer strips to the top and bottom edges. The quilt top should measure 72½" square.

Finishing the Quilt

For more details on any finishing steps, visit ShopMartingale.com/HowtoQuilt for free downloadable information.

1. Layer the quilt top with batting and backing; baste the layers together.

2. Quilt by hand or machine. The quilt shown is machine quilted with an allover pattern of on-point squares. A flower motif is stitched in the center of each square.

3. Use the coral 2¼"-wide strips to make binding and then attach the binding to the quilt.

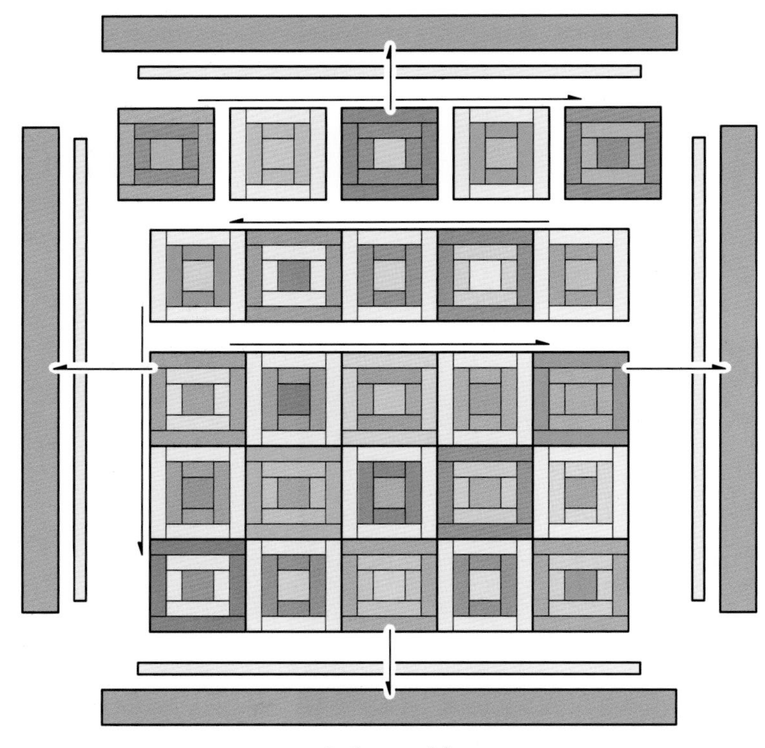

Quilt assembly

Side Door

PIECED BY SHERRI McCONNELL; QUILTED BY MARION BOTT

I have a favorite restaurant along the Oregon Coast called the Side Door Café. The food is delicious, the decor comfortable, and the outside is beautiful with greenery dancing along an overhead trellis and potted blooms in the courtyard. The restaurant's name inspired me to think about how we often miss so much beauty by concentrating on what is "out front" and not looking for the surprises that might be found in the not-so-conspicuous places.

FINISHED QUILT: 53" × 67"
FINISHED BLOCK: 12½" × 12½"

Materials

Yardage is based on 42"-wide fabric. Fat quarters measure 18" × 21".

- 12 fat quarters of assorted navy prints for blocks
- 1 yard of navy dot for blocks, sashing squares, and binding
- 2¼ yards of white solid for blocks, sashing, and inner border
- 1 yard of navy floral for outer border
- 3⅜ yards of fabric for backing
- 59" × 73" piece of batting

NAVY REVISITED

I've been wanting to make this traditional block quilt for quite some time and just couldn't settle on the fabrics. Finally, I decided it would be a lot of fun to make a companion navy quilt for one I pieced a few years ago. One of my favorite prints in that first quilt was a tiny cream dot on navy. We recently brought back that print in a newer fabric collection, and I used the navy dot as the contrast in this quilt. It still holds as much appeal to my eye.

Cutting

All measurements include ¼"-wide seam allowances.

From *each* of the navy prints, cut:
9 squares, 3" × 3" (108 total)
4 squares, 3½" × 3½" (48 total)

From the navy dot, cut:
4 strips, 3" × 42"; crosscut into 48 squares, 3" × 3"
1 strip, 2" × 42"; crosscut into 6 squares, 2" × 2"
7 strips, 2¼" × 42"

From the white solid, cut:
5 strips, 3½" × 42"; crosscut into 48 squares, 3½" × 3½"
5 strips, 3" × 42"; crosscut into 96 pieces, 1¾" × 3"
9 strips, 1¾" × 42"; crosscut into 192 squares, 1¾" × 1¾"
12 strips, 2" × 42"; crosscut 6 *of the strips* into 17 strips, 2" × 13"

From the navy floral, cut:
6 strips, 5" × 42".

Making the Blocks

Press seam allowances in the directions indicated by the arrows.

1. Draw a diagonal line from corner to corner on the wrong side of the white 3½" squares. Layer a marked square on a navy print 3½" square, right sides together. Sew ¼" from both sides of the drawn line. Cut the unit apart on the marked line to make two half-square-triangle units. Trim the units to measure 3" square, including seam allowances. Make 12 sets of eight matching units.

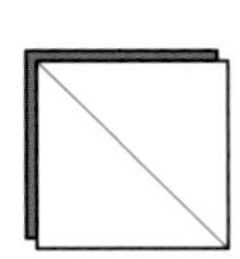

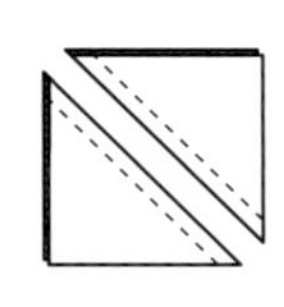

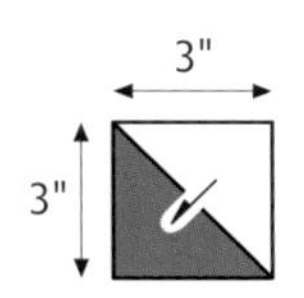

Make 12 sets of 8 matching units.

2. Lay out two navy print 3" squares and two half-square-triangle units in two rows of two. The navy print should be the same in all of the units and squares. Sew the units and squares into rows. Join the rows to make a corner unit measuring 5½" square, including seam allowances. Make 12 sets of four matching units.

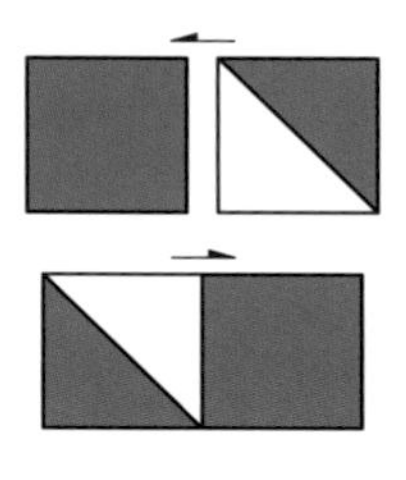

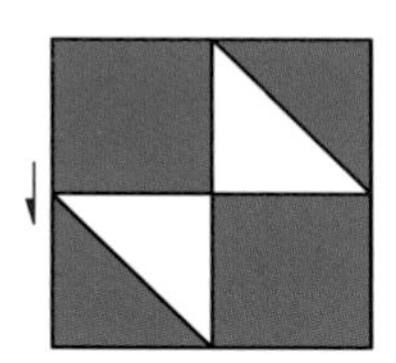

Make 12 sets of 4 matching units, 5½" × 5½".

3. Draw a diagonal line from corner to corner on the wrong side of the white 1¾" squares. Place marked squares on opposite corners of a navy dot 3" square. Sew on the marked line. Trim the excess corner fabric, ¼" from the stitched line. Place marked squares on the remaining corners of the square. Sew and trim as before to make a square-in-a-square unit measuring 3" square, including seam allowances. Make 48 units.

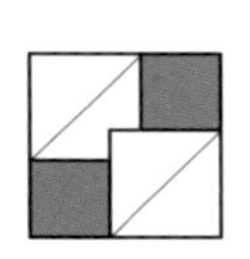

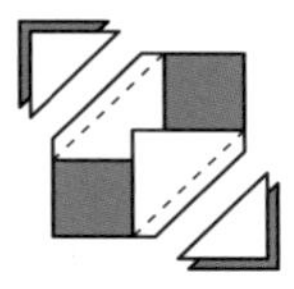

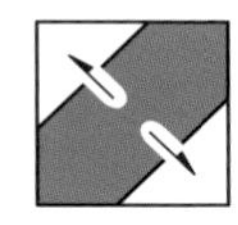

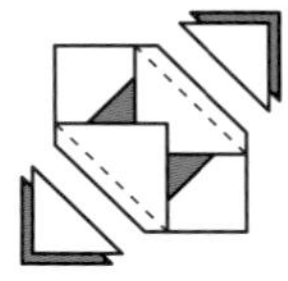

Make 48 units, 3" × 3".

4. Sew two white 1¾" × 3" pieces to opposite sides of a square-in-a-square unit to make a side unit measuring 3" × 5½", including seam allowances. Make 48 units.

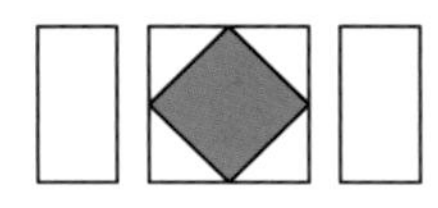

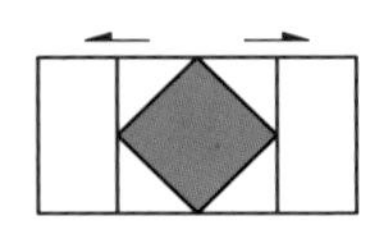

Make 48 units, 3" × 5½".

5. Lay out four matching corner units, four side units, and one navy print 3" square in three rows. The navy square should match the corner units. Sew the units and square into rows. Join the rows to make a block measuring 13" square, including seam allowances. Make 12 blocks.

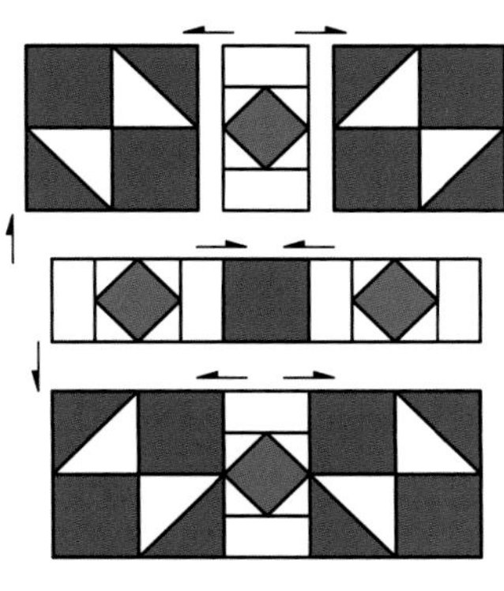

Make 12 blocks,
13" × 13".

Assembling the Quilt Top

1. Join three blocks and two white 2" × 13" strips to make a block row. Make four rows measuring 13" × 41", including seam allowances.

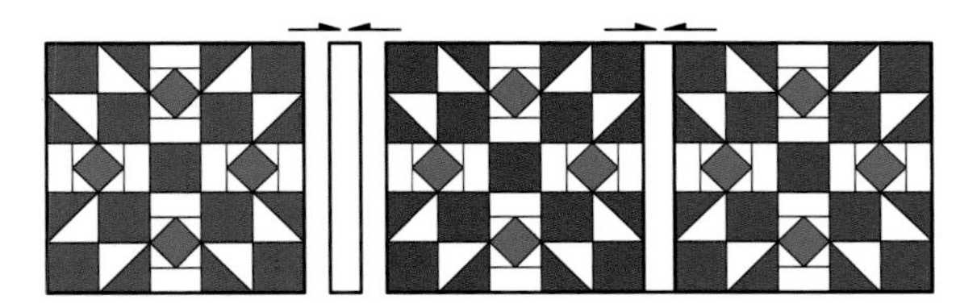

Make 4 rows, 13" × 41".

2. Join three white 2" × 13" strips and two navy dot 2" squares to make a sashing row. Make three rows measuring 2" × 41", including seam allowances.

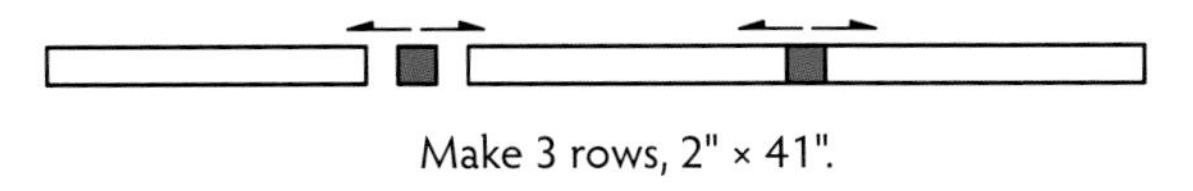

Make 3 rows, 2" × 41".

3. Join the block rows alternately with the sashing rows as shown in the quilt assembly diagram above right. The quilt-top center should measure 41" × 55", including seam allowances.

4. Join the remaining white 2"-wide strips end to end. From the strip, cut two 55"-long and two 44"-long strips. Sew the longer strips to opposite sides of the quilt top. Sew the shorter strips to the top and bottom edges. The quilt-top center should measure 44" × 58", including seam allowances.

5. Join the navy floral 5"-wide strips end to end. From the pieced strip, cut two 58"-long strips and two 53"-long strips. Sew the longer strips to opposite sides of the quilt top. Sew the shorter strips to the top and bottom edges. The quilt-top center should measure 53" × 67".

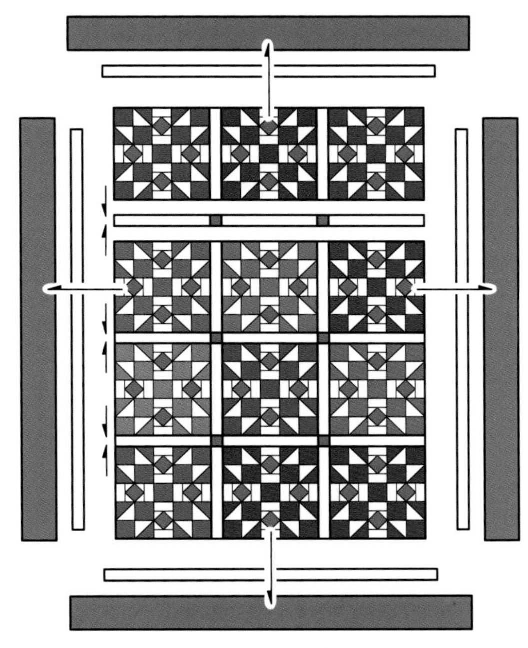

Quilt assembly

Finishing the Quilt

For more details on any finishing steps, visit ShopMartingale.com/HowtoQuilt for free downloadable information.

1. Layer the quilt top with batting and backing; baste the layers together.

2. Quilt by hand or machine. The quilt shown is machine quilted with an allover clamshell pattern.

3. Use the navy dot 2¼"-wide strips to make binding and then attach the binding to the quilt.

Mini Log Cabins Pillow

PIECED BY SHERRI MCCONNELL; QUILTED BY MARION BOTT

The Log Cabin is one of my favorite quilt blocks. In my book* Labor of Love: Scrappy Quilts at the Heart of Home *(Martingale, 2020), I shared one of my favorite Log Cabin designs: a scrappy quilt with low-volume background fabrics in my favorite setting. So last year, when I started making mini Log Cabin blocks just for fun, I decided I'd better think of a good way to use them. This pillow is my first project using these mini blocks, and I'm sure there will be several more . . . I'm addicted!

FINISHED PILLOW: 16½" × 16½"
FINISHED BLOCK: 4" × 4"

Materials

Yardage is based on 42"-wide fabric.

* ⅛ yard *total* of assorted yellow prints for block centers
* ⅜ yard *total* of assorted light prints for blocks
* ½ yard *total* of assorted medium and dark prints (referred to collectively as "dark") for blocks
* ⅝ yard of muslin for quilt-sandwich backing
* ⅓ yard of cream floral for pillow back
* ⅛ yard of green floral for zipper flap
* ¼ yard of purple print for binding
* 20" × 20" square of batting
* 16" × 16" pillow form
* 20" zipper

MIX AND MATCH

In order to unify the scrappy blocks, I chose a variety of yellow prints for the cabin centers. Then I really had fun mixing and matching prints for each block. In some of the blocks, I used the same print for both pieces in the same "round," while in others I used different prints from the same color family.

Cutting

All measurements include ¼"-wide seam allowances.

From the yellow prints, cut a *total* of:
16 squares, 1½" × 1½"

From the light prints, cut a *total* of:
16 A pieces, 1" × 1½"
16 B pieces, 1" × 2"
16 E pieces, 1" × 2½"
16 F pieces, 1" × 3"
16 I pieces, 1" × 3½"
16 J pieces, 1" × 4"

From the dark prints, cut a *total* of:
16 C pieces, 1" × 2"
16 D pieces, 1" × 2½"
16 G pieces, 1" × 3"
16 H pieces, 1" × 3½"
16 K pieces, 1" × 4"
16 L pieces, 1" × 4½"

From the muslin, cut:
1 square, 20" × 20"

From the cream floral, cut:
2 pieces, 8½" × 16½"

From the green floral, cut:
1 strip, 4" × 16½"

From the purple print, cut:
2 strips, 2¼" × 42"

CHOOSE TWO COLORS

While this pillow is stunning with a scrappy variety of light, medium, and dark prints, it would also be absolutely beautiful made in a two-color version.

Making the Blocks

Press seam allowances in the directions indicated by the arrows.

1. Sew an A piece to the left side of a yellow square. Sew a B piece to the top of the square. Make 16 units measuring 2" square, including seam allowances.

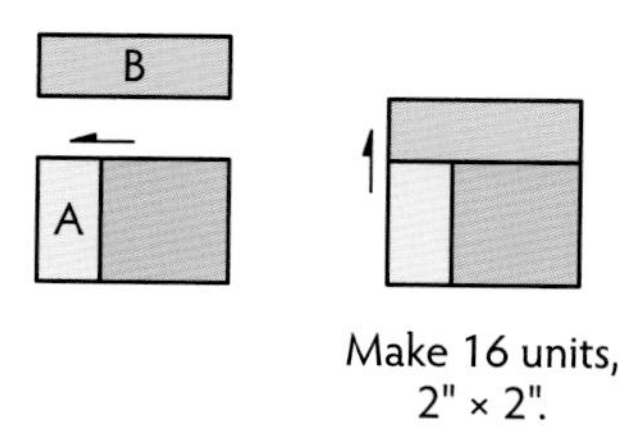

Make 16 units, 2" × 2".

2. Sew a C piece to the right edge of the unit and a D piece to the bottom of the unit. Make 16 units measuring 2½" square, including seam allowances.

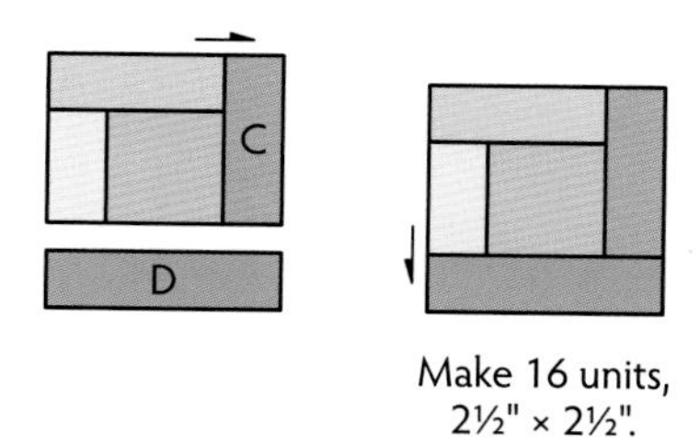

Make 16 units, 2½" × 2½".

3. In the same way, sew E–H pieces, in alphabetical order, to the unit from step 2. Make 16 units measuring 3½" square, including seam allowances.

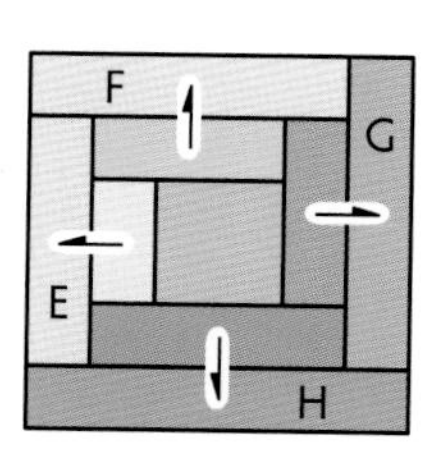

Make 16 units, 3½" × 3½".

4. Add I–L pieces to the unit, in alphabetical order, to make a block. Make 16 blocks measuring 4½" square, including seam allowances.

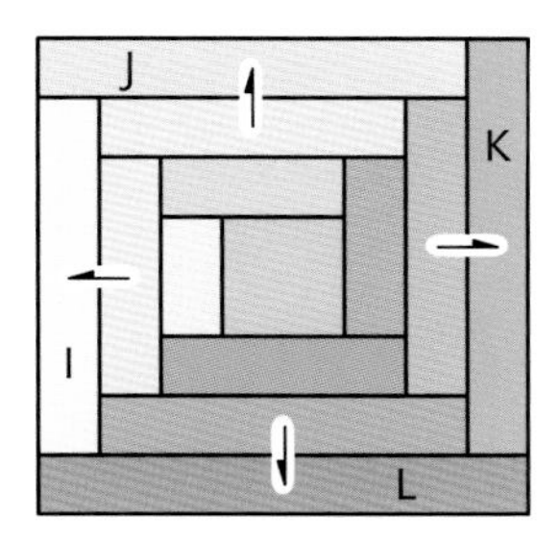

Make 16 blocks, 4½" × 4½".

SPEED UP THE PROCESS

There's more than one way to piece these fun scrappy blocks. You can lay out all of the pieces for one block and sew one at a time, or you can make the blocks faster by chain piecing. Here's how to do it: I start by cutting all of the required pieces. Next, I organize the pieces by matching fabrics and putting them in groups on my design board. Then I chain piece the blocks to make the sewing go more quickly. For this pillow top, I pieced the blocks in groups of three to five so I wouldn't mix up the pieces. I also took pictures as a reference in case anything got out of order.

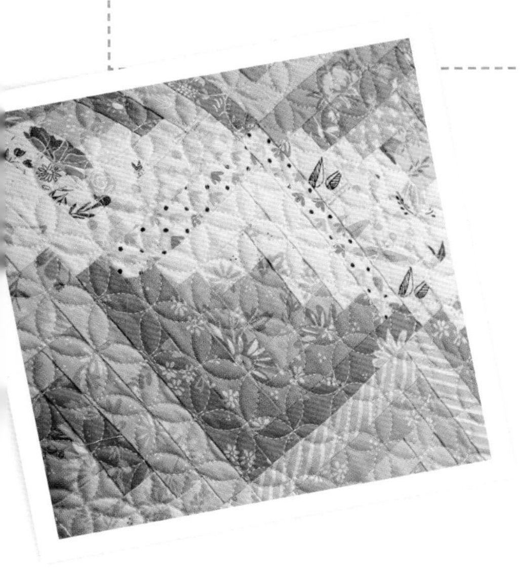

Assembling the Pillow Top

Lay out the blocks in four rows of four blocks each, rotating the blocks to form light and dark diagonal lines. Sew the blocks into rows and then join the rows to make the pillow top. The pillow top should measure 16½" square, including seam allowances.

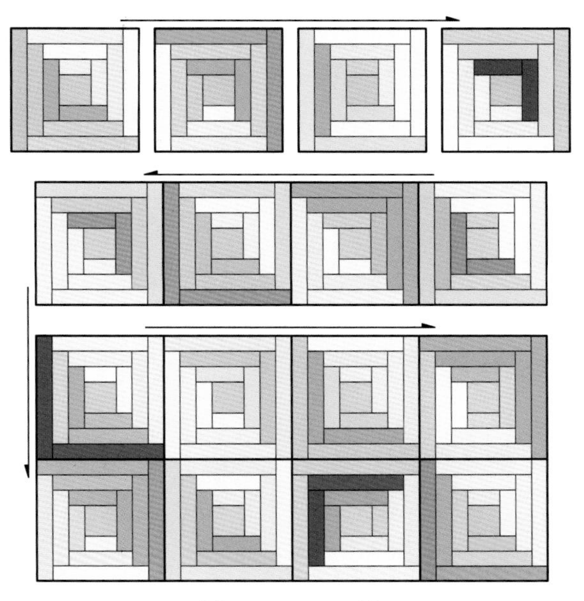

Pillow-top assembly

Finishing the Pillow

1. Layer the pillow top with batting and the muslin square; baste the layers together.

2. Quilt by hand or machine. The pillow shown is machine quilted with an allover pumpkin-seed design. Trim the batting and muslin even with the edges of the pillow top.

3. Refer to "Pillow Finishing" on page 75. Use the green strip, cream pieces, and the zipper to make the pillow back.

4. Centering the zipper, layer the pillow top and back wrong sides together. Sew around the perimeter using a ⅛" seam allowance.

5. Use the purple 2¼"-wide strips to make binding and then attach the binding to the edges of the pillow as you would a quilt.

6. Insert the pillow form through the zipper opening.

Dream

PIECED BY SHERRI McCONNELL; QUILTED BY MARION BOTT

Because the design process for fabric collections spans several months, there is plenty of time to dream of what I'll make with the new fabrics. I consider the dream stage not only an important step in creating but also one of the most fun. All quilters can experience this dream phase, and it's truly one of the benefits of becoming a quilter. Wouldn't this window seat be the perfect place to browse through quilting books to give you inspiration?

FINISHED QUILT: 53⅞" × 53⅞"
FINISHED BLOCK: 9" × 9"

Materials

Yardage is based on 42"-wide fabric.

* 13 pieces, 8" × 9" *each*, of assorted prints (3 aqua, 2 coral, 2 navy, 2 yellow, 2 pink, and 2 gray) for blocks
* 13 strips, 3" × 16" *each*, of assorted prints (3 aqua, 2 coral, 2 navy, 2 yellow, 2 pink, and 2 gray) for blocks
* 1⅝ yards of white solid for blocks and setting triangles
* ½ yard of light print for sashing
* ⅛ yard of gray diagonal stripe for sashing squares
* ⅓ yard of gold print for inner border
* ¾ yard of cream floral for outer border
* ½ yard of pink diagonal stripe for binding
* 3½ yards of fabric for backing
* 60" × 60" square of batting

SCRAPPIER LOOK

To give this quilt design a little more depth, I cut the squares for each block from one fabric and the strips from a coordinating one. I also used a low-volume (or light) print for sashing to give more texture to the quilt and to make the blocks appear to float. A bold inner border, light outer border, and diagonal stripe for binding completed the quilt with a bit of whimsy. I plan to use this quilt as a wall hanging or table topper in my home.

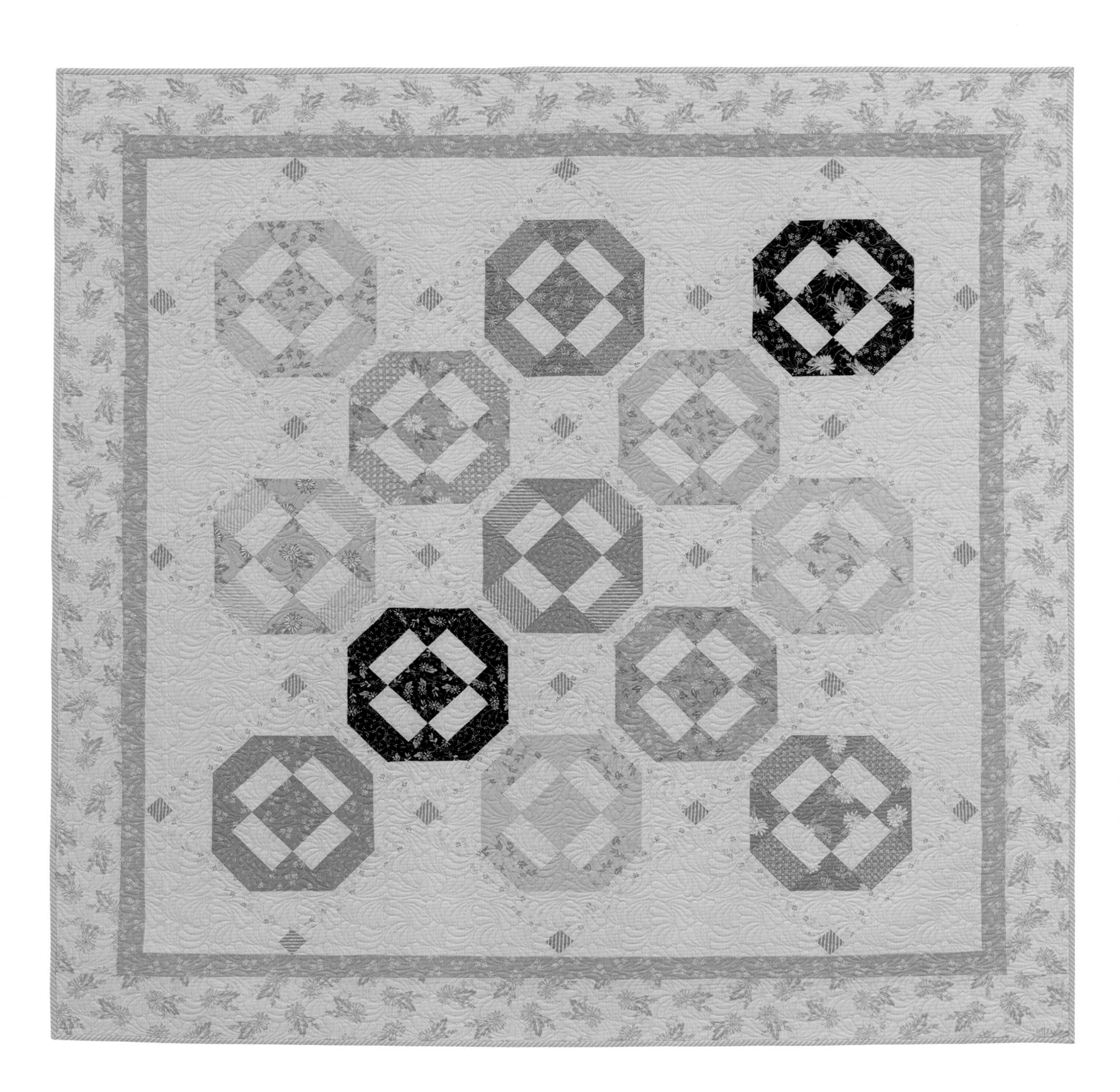

Cutting

All measurements include ¼"-wide seam allowances.

From *each* of the assorted print 8" × 9" pieces, cut:
2 squares, 4" × 4" (26 total)
1 square, 3½" × 3½" (13 total)

From *each* of the assorted print strips, cut:
1 strip, 2" × 15" (13 total)

From the white solid, cut:
1 strip, 15½" × 42"; crosscut into 2 squares, 15½" × 15½". Cut the squares into quarters diagonally to yield 8 side triangles.
1 strip, 8¾" × 42"; crosscut into 2 squares, 8¾" × 8¾". Cut the squares in half diagonally to yield 4 corner triangles.
3 strips, 4" × 42"; crosscut into 26 squares, 4" × 4"
7 strips, 2" × 42"; crosscut into 13 strips, 2" × 15"

From the light print, cut:
9 strips, 1½" × 42"; crosscut into 36 strips, 1½" × 9½"

From the gray diagonal stripe, cut:
1 strip, 1½" × 42"; crosscut into 24 squares, 1½" × 1½"

From the gold print, cut:
5 strips, 1¾" × 42"

From the cream floral, cut:
6 strips, 4" × 42"

From the pink diagonal stripe, cut:
6 strips, 2¼" × 42"

Making the Blocks

Press seam allowances in the directions indicated by the arrows.

1. Draw a diagonal line from corner to corner on the wrong side of the white 4" squares. Layer a marked square on a print 4" square, right sides together. Sew ¼" from both sides of the drawn line. Cut the unit apart on the marked line to make two half-square-triangle units. Trim the units to measure 3½" square, including seam allowances. Make 13 sets of four matching units.

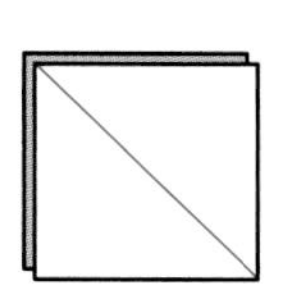
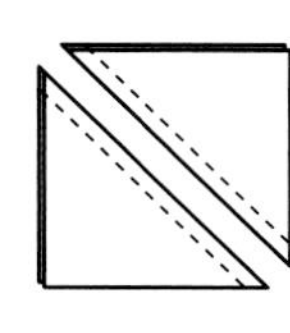
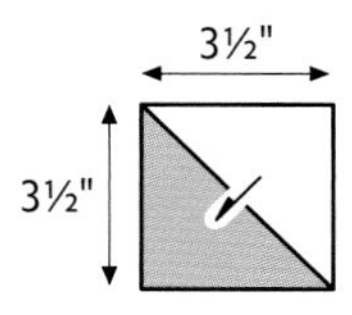

Make 13 sets of 4 matching units.

2. Sew a white 2" × 15" strip to the long side of a print 2" × 15" strip to make a strip set measuring 3½" × 15", including seam allowances. Make 13 strip sets. Cut each strip set into four segments, 3½" square (52 total).

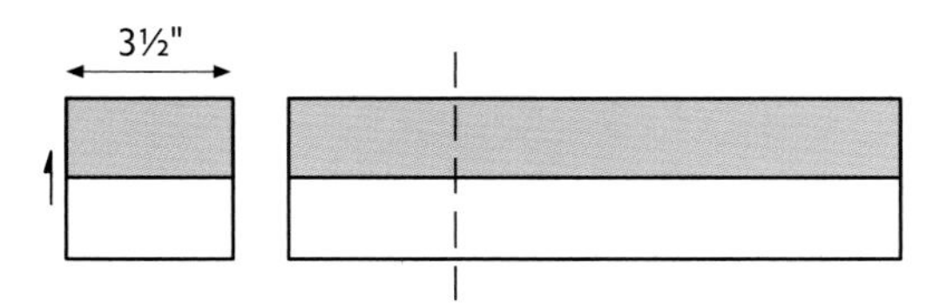

Make 13 strip sets, 3½" × 15".
Cut 4 segments from each strip set, 3½" × 3½".

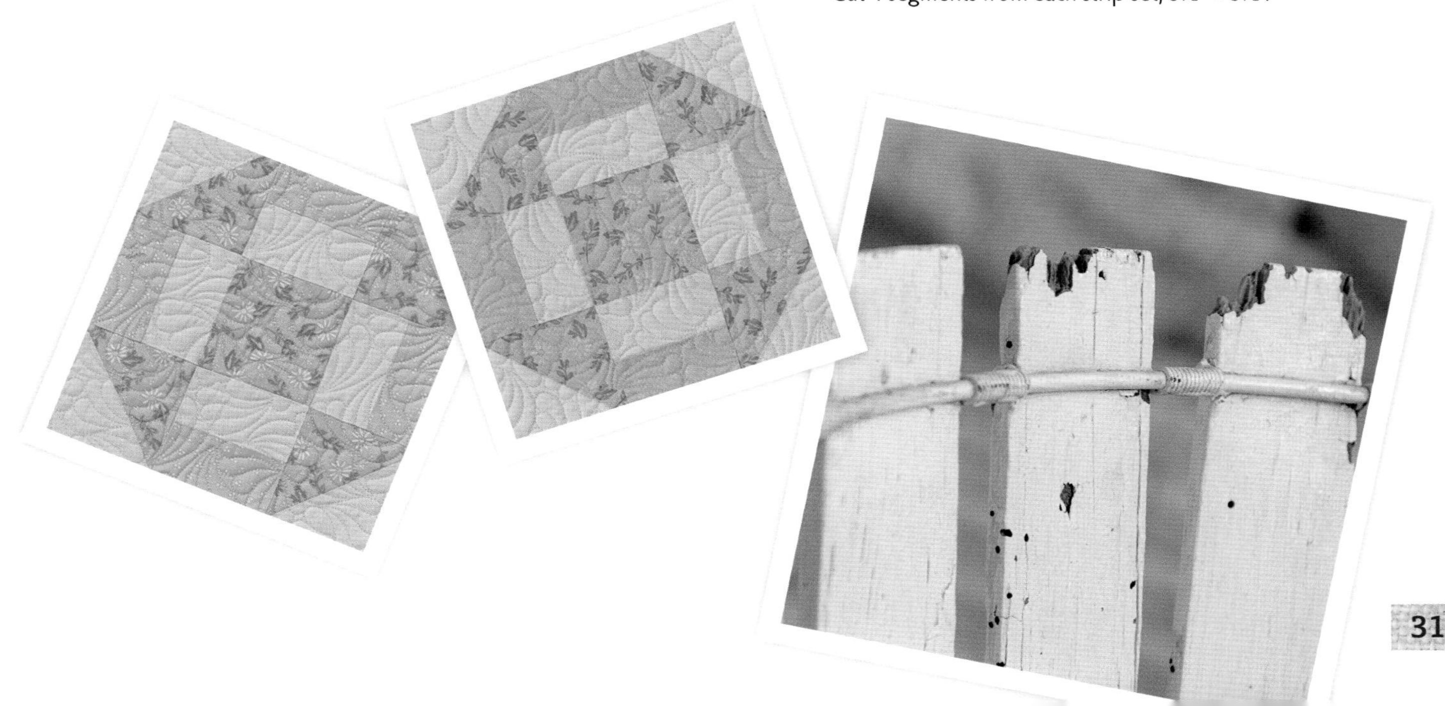

3. Lay out four half-square-triangle units, a matching 3½" print square, and four segments from step 2 in three rows of three. Sew the pieces into rows. Join the rows to make a block. Make 13 blocks measuring 9½" square, including seam allowances.

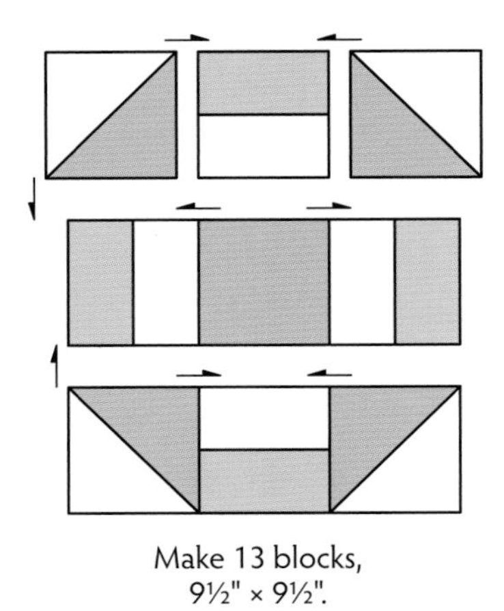

Make 13 blocks,
9½" × 9½".

Assembling the Quilt Top

1. Lay out the blocks, light 1½" × 9½" strips, gray squares, and white side and corner triangles in diagonal rows as shown in the quilt assembly diagram below. Join the light strips and gray squares to make sashing rows. Join the blocks and light strips to make block rows. Sew a sashing row to each appropriate block row, and then add the side triangles. Join the rows, adding the corner triangles last.

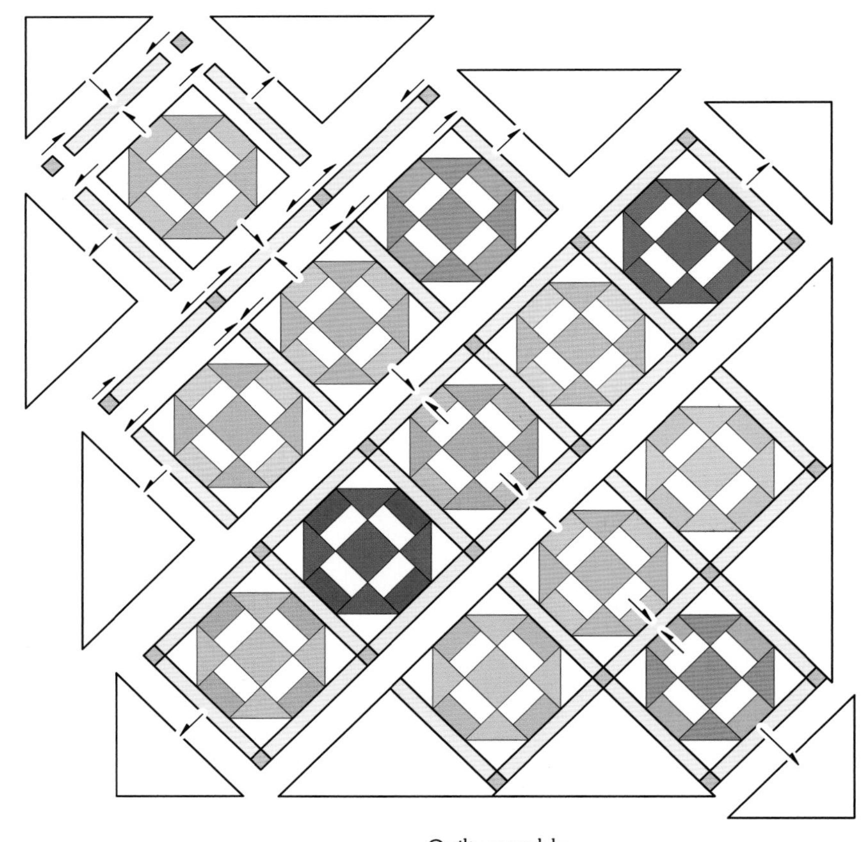

Quilt assembly

2. Trim and square up the quilt top, making sure to leave ¼" beyond the points of all gray squares for seam allowances. The quilt-top center should measure 44⅜", including seam allowances.

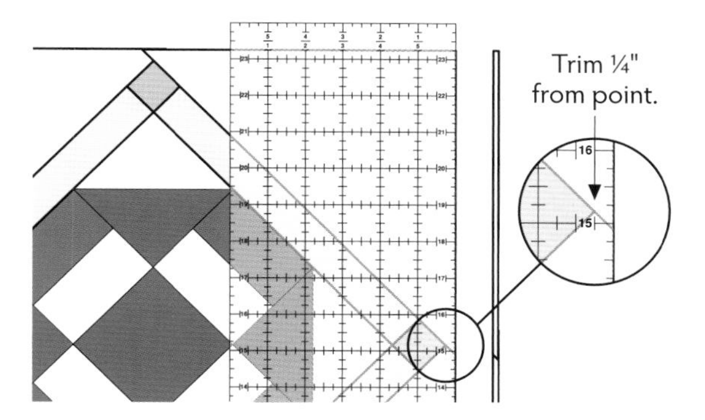

3. Join the gold strips end to end. From the pieced strip, cut two 46⅞"-long strips and two 44⅜"-long strips. Sew the shorter strips to opposite sides of the quilt center. Sew the longer strips to the top and bottom edges. Press all seam allowances toward the gold strips. The quilt top should measure 46⅞" square, including seam allowances.

4. Join the cream strips end to end. From the pieced strip, cut two 53⅞"-long strips and two 46⅞"-long strips. Sew the shorter strips to opposite sides of the quilt center. Sew the longer strips to the top and bottom edges to complete the quilt top. Press all seam allowances toward the outer border. The quilt top should measure 53⅞" square.

Finishing the Quilt

For more details on any finishing steps, visit ShopMartingale.com/HowtoQuilt for free downloadable information.

1. Layer the quilt top with batting and backing; baste the layers together.

2. Quilt by hand or machine. The quilt shown is machine quilted with an allover design of feather plumes.

3. Use the pink 2¼"-wide strips to make binding and then attach the binding to the quilt.

Backyard Blooms

PIECED BY SHERRI McCONNELL; QUILTED BY MARION BOTT

I still remember making my first Granny Square–style quilt from a tutorial I found on the Internet early in my quilting and blogging days. I fell in love with the block style then and still count it as one of my favorites. It works equally well whether set in straight rows or on point. This pattern can be used with Layer Cake squares or with your accumulated scraps. I used the Folktale fabric collection by Vanessa Goertzen of Lella Boutique.

FINISHED QUILT: 59½" × 59½"
FINISHED BLOCK: 10½" × 10½"

Materials

Yardage is based on 42"-wide fabric.

* 26 squares, 10" × 10" *each,* of assorted medium and dark prints (referred to collectively as "dark") for blocks
* ¼ yard *each* of 4 assorted light prints for blocks
* 2 yards of white solid for blocks and setting triangles
* ⅞ yard of cream floral for sashing and inner border
* ⅞ yard of blue floral for outer border and sashing squares
* ½ yard of rust print for binding
* 3¾ yards of fabric for backing
* 66" × 66" square of batting

Cutting

All measurements include ¼"-wide seam allowances. As you cut the dark and light prints, keep like fabrics together.

From *each* of 13 assorted dark squares, cut:
5 squares, 3" × 3" (65 total)

From *each* of 13 assorted dark squares, cut:
4 squares, 3" × 3" (52 total)

From *each* of 3 light prints, cut:
12 squares, 3" × 3" (36 total)

From the remaining light print, cut:
16 squares, 3" × 3"

From the white solid, cut:
1 strip, 18" × 42"; crosscut into 2 squares, 18" × 18". Cut the squares into quarters diagonally to yield 8 side triangles.
1 strip, 10" × 42"; crosscut into 2 squares, 10" × 10". Cut the squares in half diagonally to yield 4 corner triangles.
12 strips, 3" × 42"; crosscut into 156 squares, 3" × 3"

From the cream floral, cut:
18 strips, 1½" × 42"; crosscut *12 of the strips* into 36 strips, 1½" × 11"

From the blue floral, cut:
6 strips, 4" × 42"
1 strip, 1½" × 42"; crosscut into 24 squares, 1½" × 1½"

From the rust print, cut:
7 strips, 2¼" × 42"

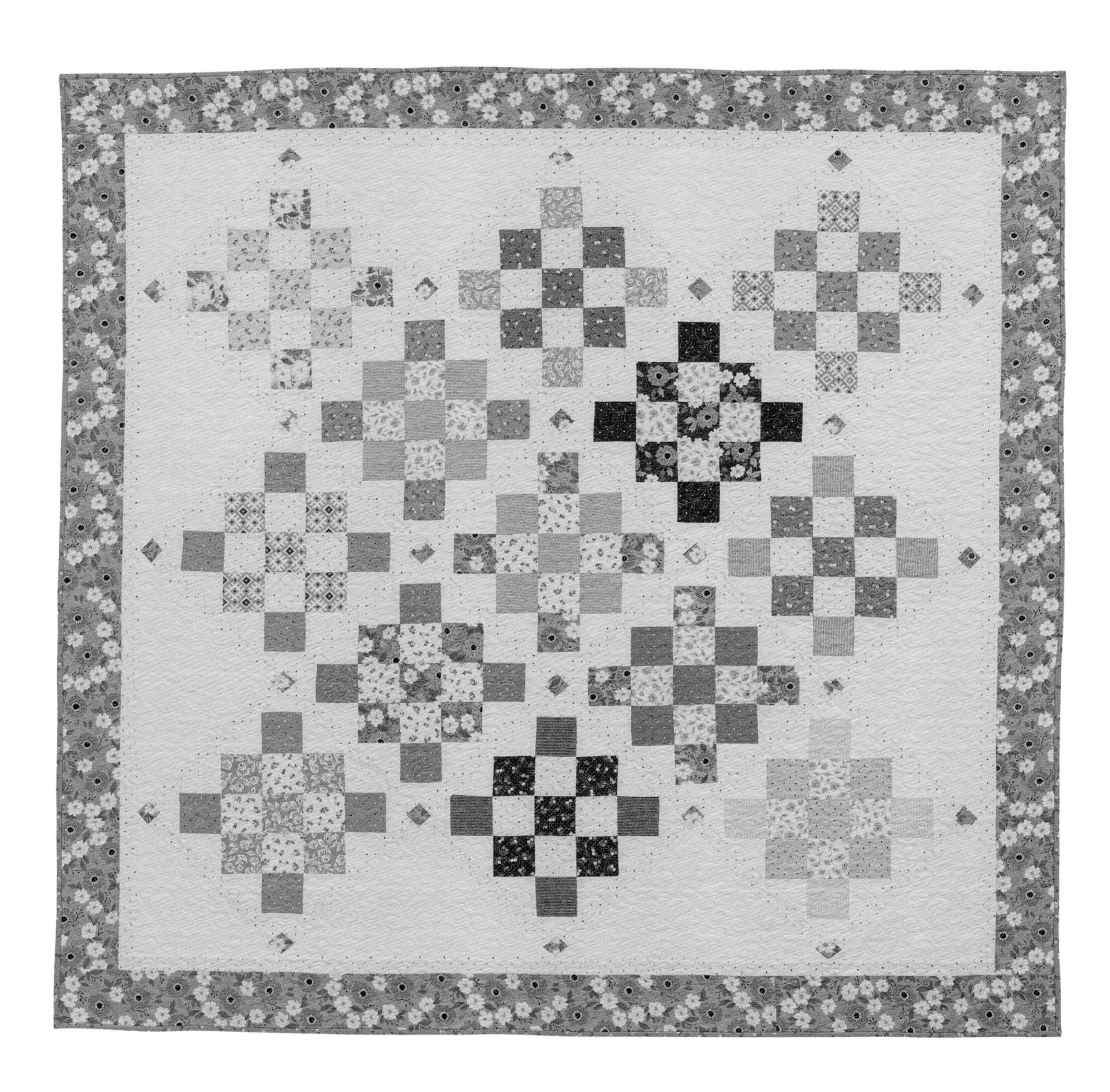

Making the Blocks

Press seam allowances in the directions indicated by the arrows.

1. Lay out five matching dark squares, four matching dark squares from a different print, four matching light squares, and 12 white 3" squares in seven diagonal rows, according to the diagram. Sew the squares into rows and then join the rows. Make 13 blocks.

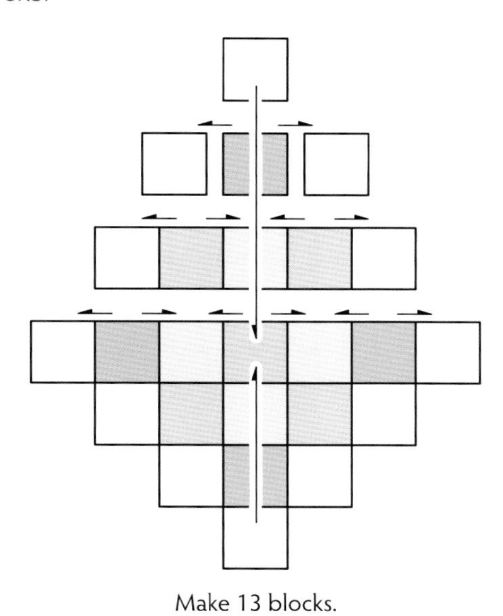

Make 13 blocks.

2. Trim and square up the blocks, making sure to leave ¼" beyond the points of all outermost print squares for seam allowances. The blocks should measure 11" square, including seam allowances.

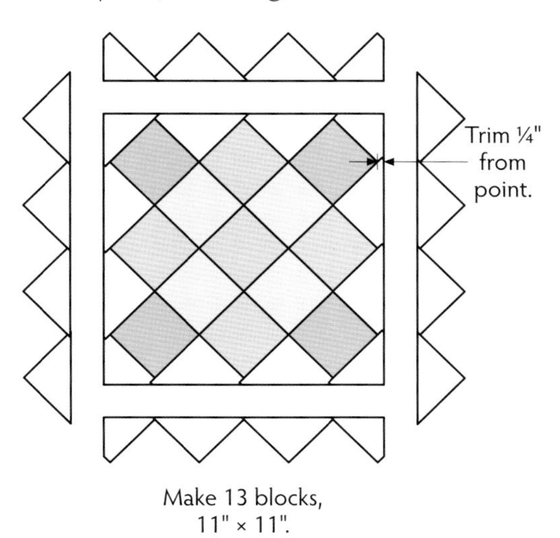

Make 13 blocks, 11" × 11".

ALL SQUARED UP

To trim the block accurately, simply align the 5½" marks on your ruler with the vertical center of the block (the 5½" line should go through the points of the center squares) and then trim. Do this on each edge and your block will be 11" square, including the seam allowances. If you have a square ruler that is 12" or larger, you can align both the vertical and horizontal 5½" lines through the center of the block and trim the right and top edges before turning the block to trim the remaining two edges.

Assembling the Quilt Top

1. Lay out the blocks, cream 1½" × 11" strips, blue squares, and white side and corner triangles in diagonal rows as shown in the quilt assembly diagram below. Join the cream strips and blue squares to make sashing rows. Join the blocks and cream strips to make block rows. Sew a sashing row to each appropriate block row, and then add the side triangles to the ends of the rows. Join the rows, adding the corner triangles last.

2. Trim and square up the quilt top, making sure to leave ¼" beyond the points of all blue squares for seam allowances. The quilt-top center should measure 50½" square, including seam allowances.

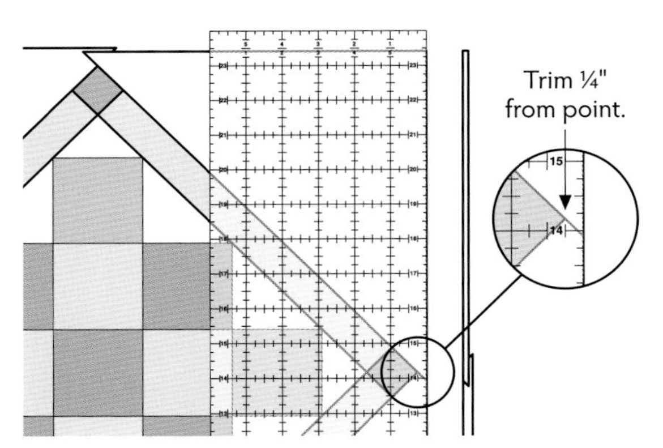

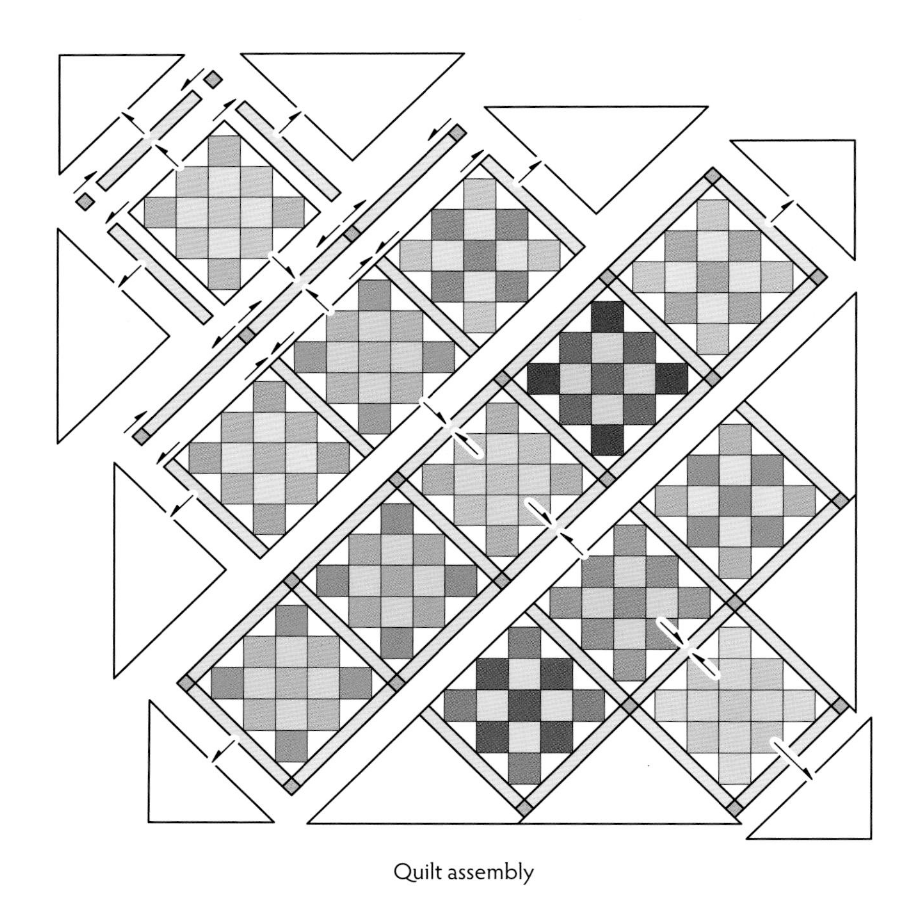

Quilt assembly

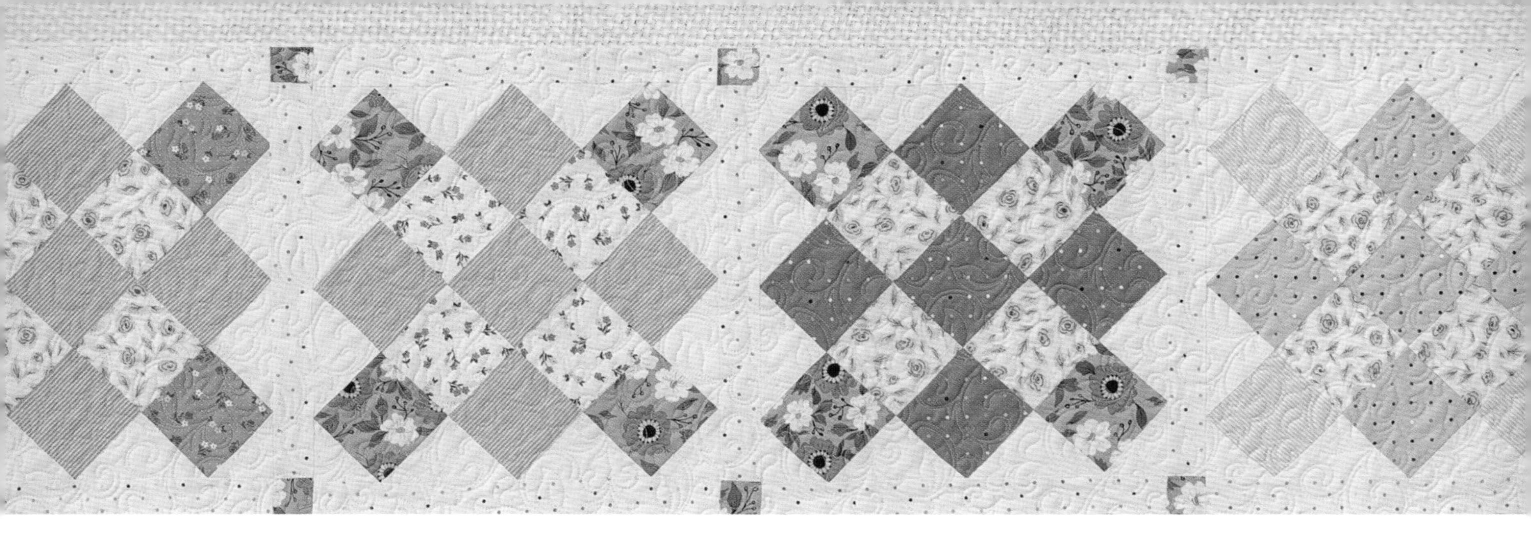

3. Join the remaining cream strips end to end. From the pieced strip, cut two 50½"-long strips and two 52½"-long strips. Sew the shorter strips to opposite sides of the quilt center. Sew the longer strips to the top and bottom edges. Press all seam allowances toward the cream strips. The quilt top should measure 52½" square, including seam allowances.

4. Join the blue 4"-wide strips end to end. From the pieced strip, cut two 52½"-long strips and two 59½"-long strips. Sew the shorter strips to opposite sides of the quilt center. Sew the longer strips to the top and bottom edges to complete the quilt top. Press all seam allowances toward the outer border. The quilt top should measure 59½" square.

Finishing the Quilt

For more details on any finishing steps, visit ShopMartingale.com/HowtoQuilt for free downloadable information.

1. Layer the quilt top with batting and backing; baste the layers together.

2. Quilt by hand or machine. The quilt shown is machine quilted with an allover pattern of leaves and swirls.

3. Use the rust 2¼"-wide strips to make binding and then attach the binding to the quilt.

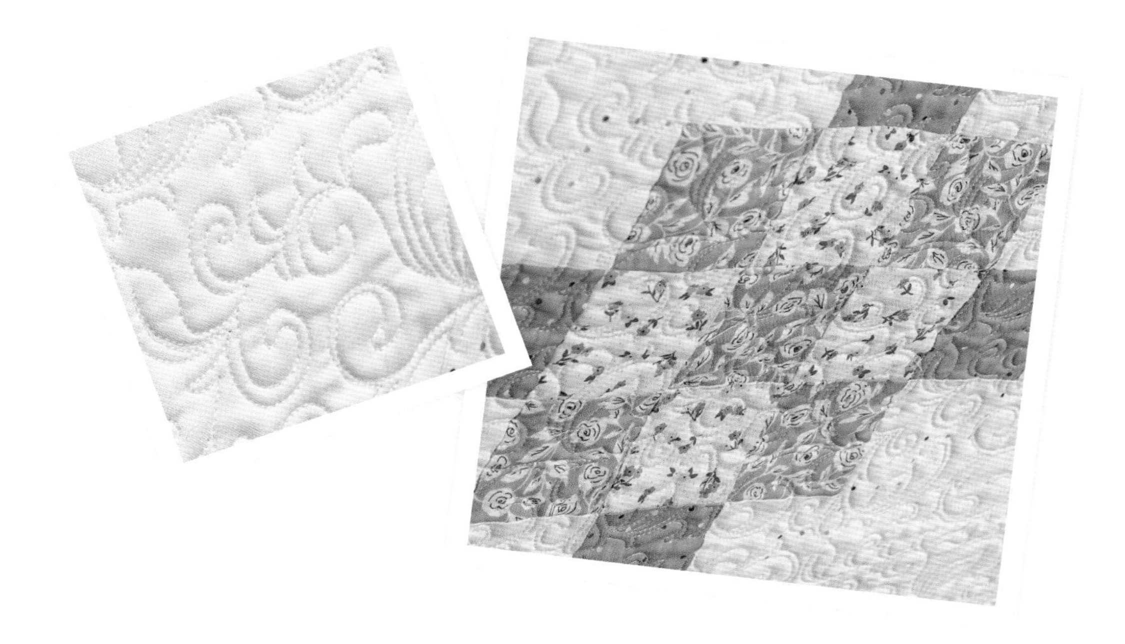

Blooming Pillow

PIECED BY SHERRI McCONNELL; QUILTED BY MARION BOTT

I've been on a mission to create pillows to coordinate with my most-used quilts. It's sort of an "every quilt should have a pillow" mantra. And while I often replicate quilt blocks in the coordinating pillows, it's also effective to use a different pattern to mix things up a bit. The simple patchwork in the Blooming Pillow both complements and accentuates the patchwork in the Backyard Blooms quilt (page 35).

FINISHED PILLOW: 18½" × 18½"
FINISHED BLOCK: 14" × 14"

Materials

Yardage is based on 42"-wide fabric. Fat eighths measure 9" × 21".

* 2 fat eighths of different light prints for block
* 4 scraps, at least 3" × 6" *each,* of assorted rust prints for block
* 3 scraps, at least 4" × 7" *each,* of assorted blue prints for block
* ⅓ yard of blue floral for block and binding
* ¼ yard of white solid for block
* ¼ yard of cream floral for border
* ¾ yard of muslin for quilt-sandwich backing
* ⅓ yard of beige print for pillow back
* ⅛ yard of rust floral for zipper flap
* 22" × 22" square of batting
* 18" × 18" pillow form
* 22" zipper

Cutting

All measurements include ¼"-wide seam allowances.

From 1 of the light prints, cut:
4 squares, 2½" × 2½"

From the remaining light print, cut:
4 pieces, 2½" × 6½"

From *each* of the rust prints, cut:
2 squares, 2½" × 2½" (8 total)

From *each* of the blue prints, cut:
2 squares, 3" × 3" (6 total)

From the blue floral, cut:
3 strips, 2¼" × 42"
2 squares, 3" × 3"
1 square, 2½" × 2½"

From the white solid, cut:
8 squares, 3" × 3"
8 squares, 2½" × 2½"

From the cream floral, cut:
2 strips, 2½" × 18½"
2 strips, 2½" × 14½"

From the muslin, cut:
1 square, 22" × 22"

Continued on page 42

Continued from page 41

From the beige print, cut:
2 pieces, 9½" × 18½"

From the rust floral, cut:
1 strip, 4" × 18½"

Making the Pillow Top

Press seam allowances in the directions indicated by the arrows.

1. Lay out two rust squares from one print, two rust squares from a different print, four matching light squares, and the blue floral 2½" square in three rows of three squares each. (Notice the matching rust squares are diagonally opposite from one another.) Sew the squares into rows. Join the rows to make a nine-patch unit measuring 6½" square, including seam allowances.

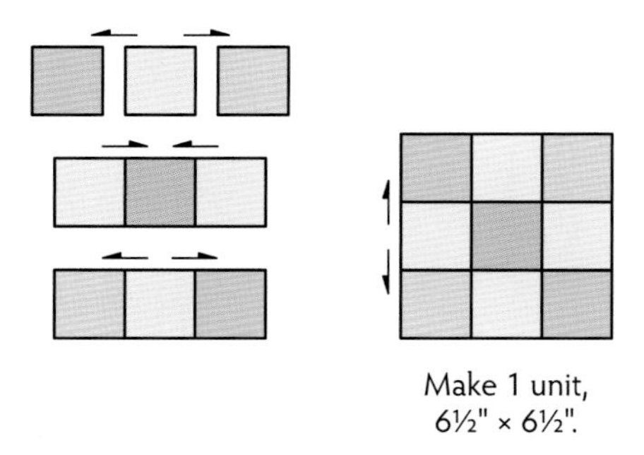

Make 1 unit, 6½" × 6½".

2. Lay out two rust squares from one print, two rust squares from a different print, four light pieces, and the nine-patch unit in three rows. Again, the matching rust squares are diagonally opposite one another. Sew into rows and then join the rows to make a center unit measuring 10½" square, including seam allowances.

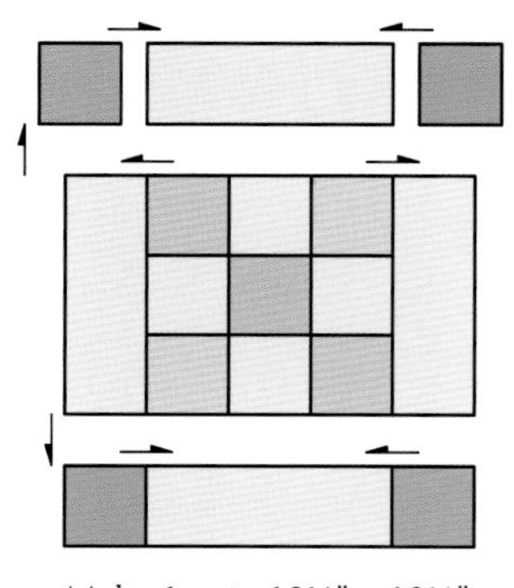

Make 1 unit, 10½" × 10½".

3. Draw a diagonal line from corner to corner on the wrong side of the white 3" squares. Layer a marked square on a blue print or floral 3" square, right sides together. Sew ¼" from both sides of the drawn line. Cut the unit apart on the marked line to make two half-square-triangle units. Trim the units to measure 2½" square, including seam allowances. Make 16 units.

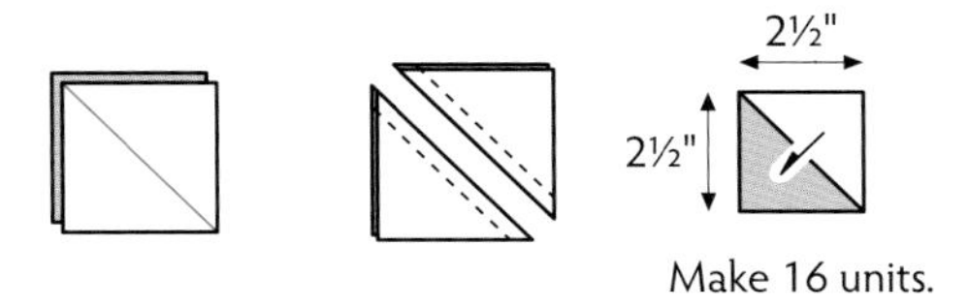

Make 16 units.

4. Lay out the white 2½" squares, half-square-triangle units, and center unit according to the diagram. The four half-square-triangle units in each corner should match. Sew the triangle units and squares into rows. Then join the rows and center unit to make a block measuring 14½" square, including seam allowances.

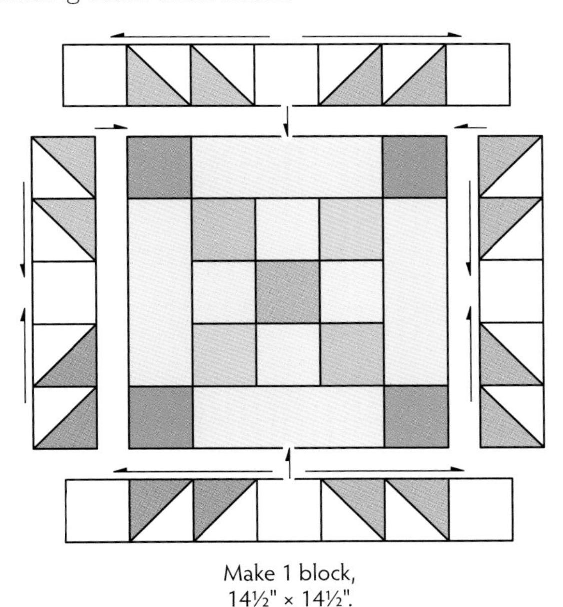
Make 1 block, 14½" × 14½".

5. Sew cream 2½" × 14½" strips to opposite sides of the block. Sew cream 2½" × 18½" strips to the top and bottom edges to complete the pillow top. The pillow top should measure 18½" square.

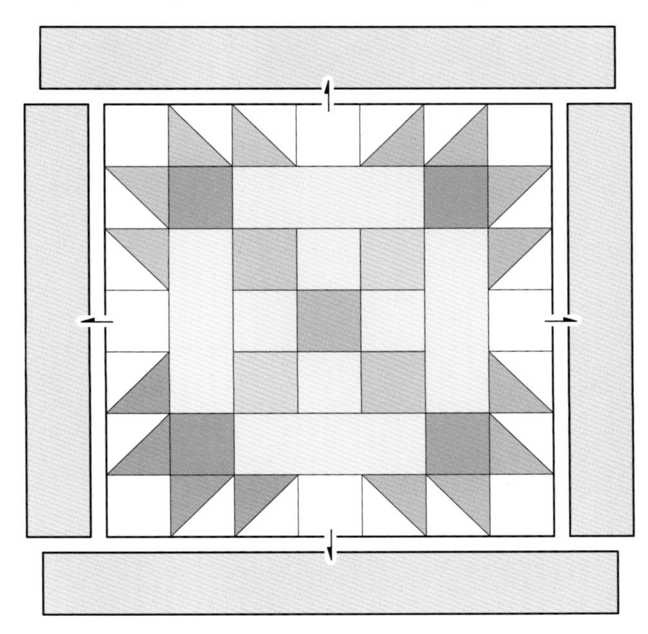
Pillow-top assembly

Finishing the Pillow

1. Layer the pillow top with batting and the muslin square; baste the layers together.

2. Quilt by hand or machine. The pillow shown is machine quilted with an allover pumpkin-seed design. Trim the batting and muslin even with the edges of the pillow top.

3. Refer to "Pillow Finishing" on page 75. Use the rust floral strip, beige rectangles, and the zipper to make the pillow back.

4. Centering the zipper, layer the pillow top and back wrong sides together. Sew around the perimeter using a ⅛" seam allowance.

5. Use the blue floral 2¼"-wide strips to make binding and then attach the binding to the edges of the pillow as you would a quilt.

6. Insert the pillow form through the zipper opening.

Al Fresco Runner

PIECED BY SHERRI McCONNELL; QUILTED BY MARION BOTT

I love using a handful of blocks to make runners. It's fun to mix and match color combinations and change runners out seasonally. The Al Fresco Runner is pieced with some fabrics that say "fall" to me but are perfectly suited for any time of year.

FINISHED RUNNER: 14½" × 54½"
FINISHED BLOCK: 10" × 10"

Materials

Yardage is based on 42"-wide fabric. Fat eighths measure 9" × 21".

- 10 fat eighths of assorted prints for blocks and binding
- ⅞ yard of cream solid for blocks and border
- 1¼ yards of fabric for backing
- 21" × 61" piece of batting

Cutting

All measurements include ¼"-wide seam allowances.

From *each* of 5 assorted prints, cut:
6 squares, 3" × 3" (30 total)
1 strip, 2¼" × 21" (5 total)

From *each* of the remaining 5 assorted prints, cut:
4 squares, 2½" × 2½" (20 total)
1 strip, 2¼" × 21" (5 total, 2 are extra)

From the cream solid, cut:
3 strips, 3" × 42"; crosscut into 30 squares, 3" × 3"
7 strips, 2½" × 42"; crosscut *4 of the strips* into:
  2 strips, 2½" × 10½"
  45 squares, 2½" × 2½"

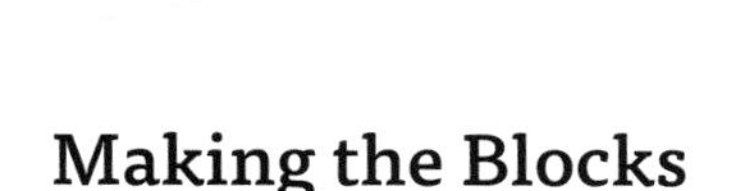

Making the Blocks

Press seam allowances in the directions indicated by the arrows.

1. Draw a diagonal line from corner to corner on the wrong side of the cream 3" squares. Layer a marked square on a print 3" square, right sides together. Sew ¼" from both sides of the drawn line. Cut the unit apart on the marked line to make two half-square-triangle units. Trim the units to measure 2½" square, including seam allowances. Make five sets of 12 matching units.

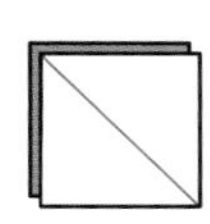
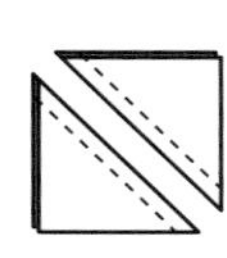
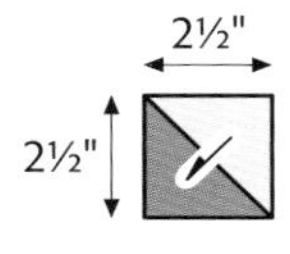

Make 5 sets of 12 matching units.

2. Lay out nine cream 2½" squares, four matching print 2½" squares, and 12 matching half-square-triangle units in five rows of five, according to the diagram. Sew the squares and units into rows. Join the rows to make a block measuring 10½" square, including seam allowances. Make five blocks.

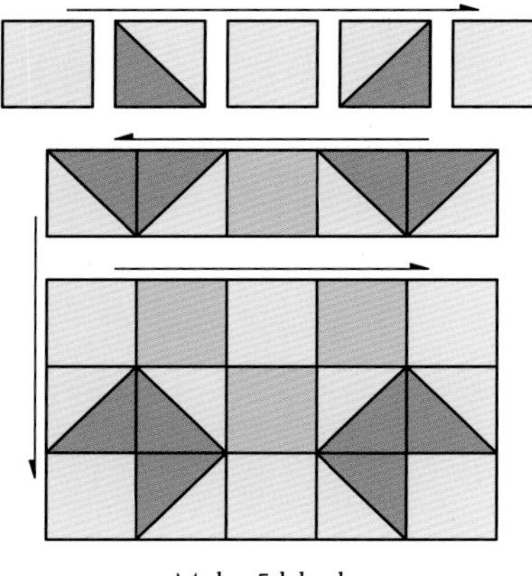

Make 5 blocks,
10½" × 10½".

Assembling the Runner

1. Referring to the runner assembly diagram below, join the blocks to make a row measuring 10½" × 50½", including seam allowances.

2. Sew the cream 2½" × 10½" strips to the short ends of the runner. Join the remaining cream 2½"-wide strips end to end. From the pieced strip, cut two 54½"-long strips and sew them to the long sides of the runner. The runner should measure 14½" × 54½".

Finishing the Runner

For more details on any finishing steps, visit ShopMartingale.com/HowtoQuilt for free downloadable information.

1. Layer the runner top with batting and backing; baste the layers together.

2. Quilt by hand or machine. The runner shown is machine quilted with an allover pattern of swirls.

3. Use the print 2¼"-wide strips to make a scrappy binding and then attach the binding to the runner.

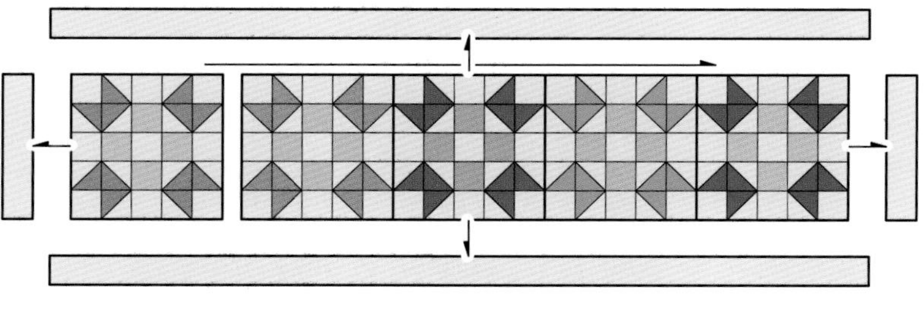

Runner assembly

Garden Blooms Pillow

PIECED BY SHERRI McCONNELL; QUILTED BY MARION BOTT

I'd been wanting to make a fun decor pillow for my home for quite some time. I think you'll find Garden Blooms Pillow to be a perfect size to use as an accent pillow on a bed, chair, sofa, or bench. I used a combination of my favorite citrine yellow and gray prints; what colors will you choose?

FINISHED PILLOW: 28½" × 17¼"
FINISHED BLOCK: 3" × 3"

Materials

Yardage is based on 42"-wide fabric.

- ¼ yard of gray floral for blocks
- ⅓ yard of yellow floral for blocks and border
- ⅜ yard of white solid for blocks and setting triangles
- ⅞ yard of white floral for sashing and pillow back
- ⅛ yard of gray diagonal stripe for sashing squares
- 1⅓ yards of muslin for quilt-sandwich backing
- ¼ yard of pink print for zipper flap
- ¼ yard of gray print for binding
- 2 pieces of batting, 21" × 32" *each*
- 17" × 28" pillow form
- 32" zipper

FOCAL POINT

The gray fabrics in this pillow serve as a neutral canvas and allow the citrine yellows, soft corals, and greens in the prints to really stand out. By piecing more gray Nine Patch blocks than citrine blocks, the center blocks and the border become the focal point of the pillow.

Cutting

All measurements include ¼"-wide seam allowances.

From the gray floral, cut:

3 strips, 1½" × 42"; crosscut into:
- 2 strips, 1½" × 26"
- 1 strip, 1½" × 14"

From the yellow floral, cut:

1 strip, 1½" × 42"; crosscut into:
- 1 strip, 1½" × 12"
- 2 strips, 1½" × 6"

3 strips, 2½" × 42"; crosscut into:
- 2 strips, 2½" × 28½"
- 2 strips, 2½" × 13¼"

From the white solid, cut:

3 strips, 1½" × 42"; crosscut into:
- 1 strip, 1½" × 26"
- 2 strips, 1½" × 14"
- 2 strips, 1½" × 12"
- 1 strip, 1½" × 6"

2 squares, 7" × 7"; cut into quarters diagonally to yield 8 side triangles

2 squares, 4½" × 4½"; cut in half diagonally to yield 4 corner triangles

From the white floral, cut:

3 strips, 1½" × 42"; crosscut into 32 pieces, 1½" × 3½"

1 piece, 21" × 32"

From the gray diagonal stripe, cut:

1 strip, 1½" × 42"; crosscut into 22 squares, 1½" × 1½"

From the muslin, cut:

2 pieces, 21" × 32"

From the pink print, cut:

1 strip, 4" × 28½"

From the gray print, cut:

3 strips, 2¼" × 42"

Making the Blocks

Press seam allowances in the directions indicated by the arrows.

1. Sew a gray floral 1½" × 26" strip to each long side of the white solid 1½" × 26" strip to make a strip set measuring 3½" × 26", including seam allowances. Cut the strip set into 16 segments, 1½" × 3½".

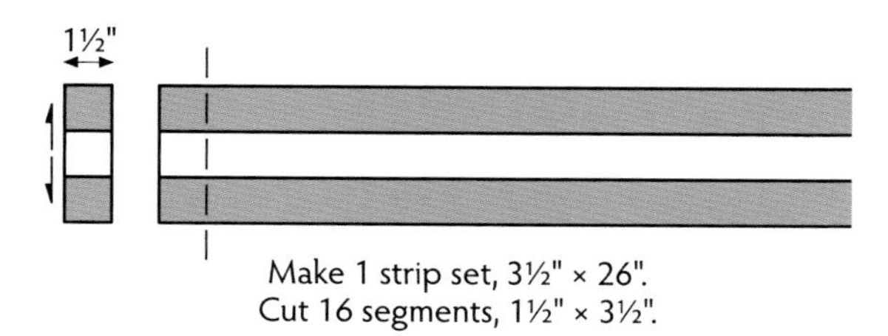

Make 1 strip set, 3½" × 26".
Cut 16 segments, 1½" × 3½".

2. Sew a white solid 1½" × 14" strip to each long side of the gray floral 1½" × 14" strip to make a strip set measuring 3½" × 14", including seam allowances. Cut the strip set into eight segments, 1½" × 3½".

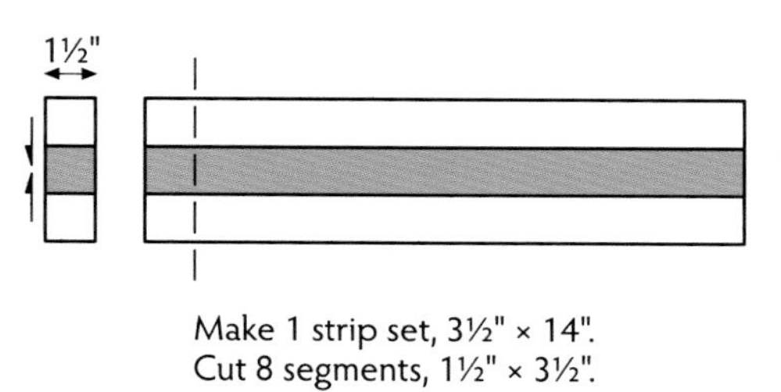

Make 1 strip set, 3½" × 14".
Cut 8 segments, 1½" × 3½".

3. Join two segments from step 1 and one segment from step 2 to make a gray Nine Patch block. Make eight blocks measuring 3½" square, including seam allowances.

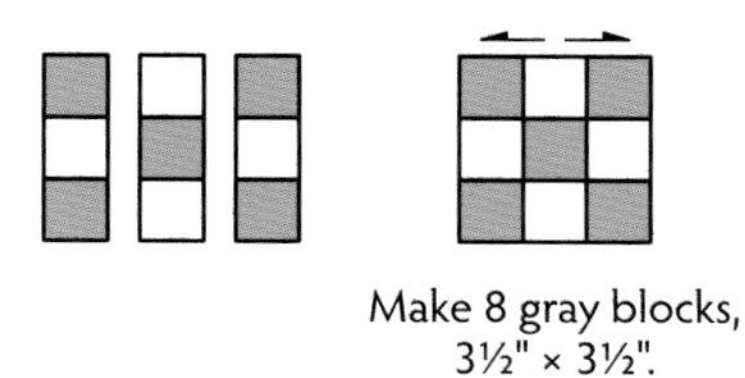

Make 8 gray blocks, 3½" × 3½".

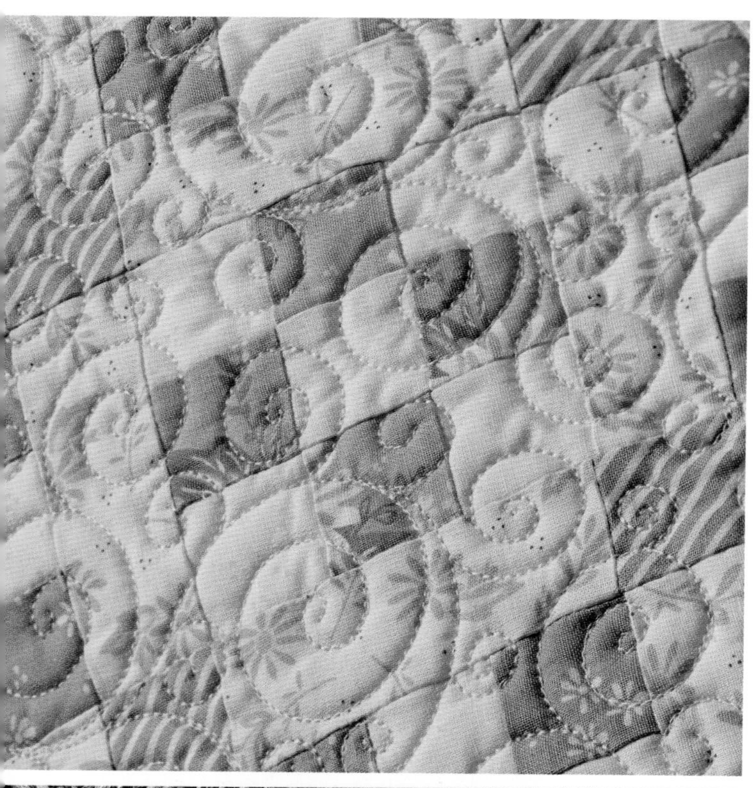

4. Sew a white solid 1½" × 12" strip to each long side of the yellow floral 1½" × 12" strip to make a strip set measuring 3½" × 12", including seam allowances. Cut the strip set into six segments, 1½" × 3½".

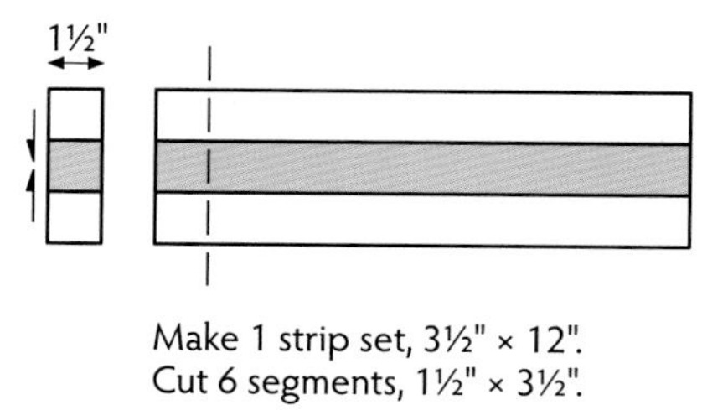

Make 1 strip set, 3½" × 12".
Cut 6 segments, 1½" × 3½".

5. Sew a yellow floral 1½" × 6" strip to each long side of the white solid 1½" × 6" strip to make a strip set measuring 3½" × 6", including seam allowances. Cut the strip set into three segments, 1½" × 3½".

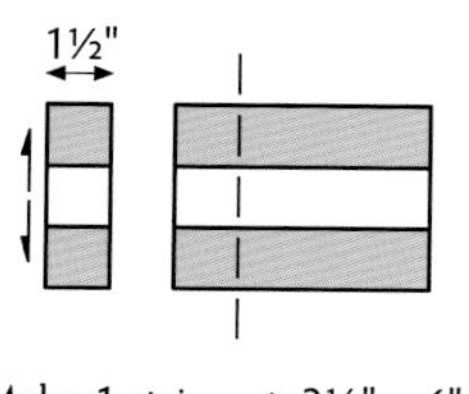

Make 1 strip set, 3½" × 6".
Cut 3 segments, 1½" × 3½".

6. Join two segments from step 4 and one segment from step 5 to make a yellow Nine Patch block. Make three blocks measuring 3½" square, including seam allowances.

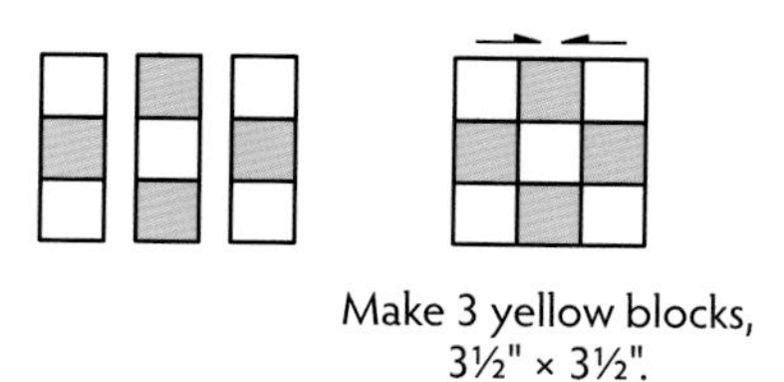

Make 3 yellow blocks,
3½" × 3½".

Assembling the Pillow Top

1. Lay out the gray blocks, yellow blocks, white floral strips, gray stripe squares, and white solid side and corner triangles in diagonal rows as shown in the pillow-top assembly diagram on page 51. Join the white strips and gray squares to make sashing rows. Join the blocks and white pieces to make the block rows. Sew a sashing row to the top of each appropriate block row, and then add side triangles. Join the rows, adding the corner triangles last.

2. Trim and square up the pillow top, making sure to leave ¼" beyond the points of all gray squares for seam allowances. The pillow-top center should measure 13¼" × 24½", including seam allowances.

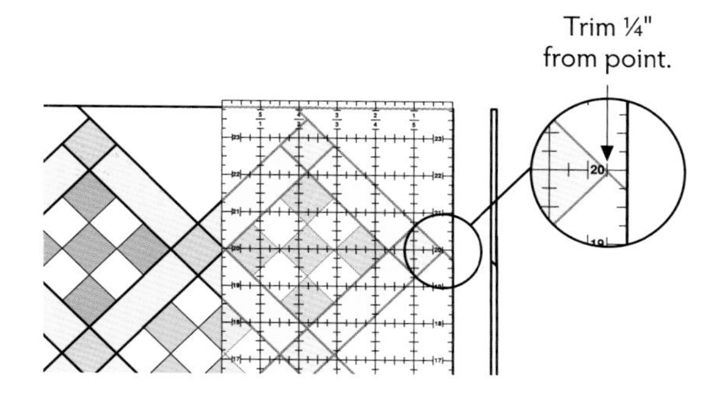

3. Sew the yellow floral 2½" × 13¼" strips to the short ends of the pillow-top center. Sew the yellow floral 2½" × 28½" strips to the long edges of the pillow top. Press all seam allowances toward the yellow strips. The pillow top should measure 28½" × 17¼".

Finishing the Pillow

1. Layer the pillow top with batting and a muslin piece; baste the layers together. For the pillow back, layer the white floral 21" × 32" piece with batting and the remaining muslin piece; baste the layers together.

2. Quilt by hand or machine. The pillow top and back are both machine quilted with an allover swirl design.

3. Cut the quilted pillow back into two 9" × 28½" pieces.

4. Refer to "Pillow Finishing" on page 75. Use the pink strip, quilted pieces from step 4, and the zipper to make the pillow back.

5. Centering the zipper, layer the pillow top and back wrong sides together. Sew around the perimeter using a ⅛" seam allowance.

6. Use the gray print 2¼"-wide strips to make binding and then attach the binding to the edges of the pillow as you would a quilt.

7. Insert the pillow form through the zipper opening.

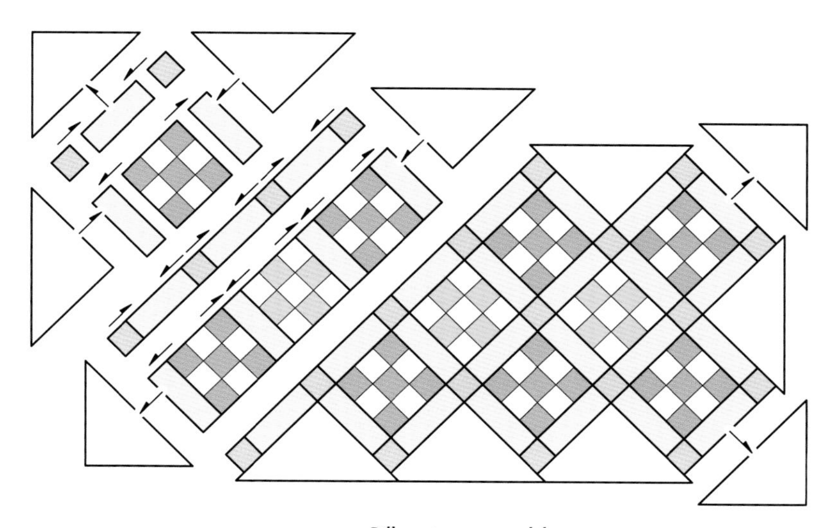

Pillow-top assembly

Hearts at Home Quilt

PIECED BY SHERRI McCONNELL; QUILTED BY MARION BOTT

I love Heart blocks and feel like heart quilts and projects shouldn't be used only for Valentine's Day. The Hearts at Home Quilt and Runner (pages 53 and 59) would, of course, be wonderful in Valentine-themed fabrics. But these projects add a happy touch regardless of the fabrics used. Whether you use this small quilt as a table topper or wall hanging, it's sure to brighten your home. I made this quilt using our Balboa collection.

FINISHED QUILT: 27½" × 27½"
FINISHED BLOCK: 6" × 6"

Materials

Yardage is based on 42"-wide fabric.

* ⅝ yard of white solid for blocks, sashing, and middle border
* 4 squares, 8" × 8" *each,* of assorted blue prints for blocks
* 1 piece, 7" × 10", of pink stripe for sashing
* ¼ yard of green print for sashing and pieced border
* ⅜ yard of cream floral for outer border
* ¼ yard of pink print for binding
* 1 yard of fabric for backing
* 32" × 32" square of batting

Cutting

All measurements include ¼"-wide seam allowances.

From the white solid, cut:

1 strip, 3½" × 42"; crosscut into 8 squares, 3½" × 3½"
2 strips, 3" × 42"; crosscut into 24 squares, 3" × 3"
1 strip, 2½" × 42"; crosscut into 16 squares, 2½" × 2½"
4 strips, 1½" × 42"; crosscut into:
- 2 strips, 1½" × 22½"
- 2 strips, 1½" × 20½"
- 16 squares, 1½" × 1½"

From *each* of the blue prints, cut:

2 pieces, 3½" × 6½" (8 total)

From the pink stripe, cut:

6 squares, 3" × 3"

From the green print, cut:

2 strips, 3" × 42"; crosscut into 18 squares, 3" × 3"

From the cream floral, cut:

4 strips, 3" × 42"; crosscut into:
- 2 strips, 3" × 27½"
- 2 strips, 3" × 22½"

From the pink print, cut:

3 strips, 2¼" × 42"

Making the Blocks

Press seam allowances in the directions indicated by the arrows.

1. Draw a diagonal line from corner to corner on the wrong side of the white 3½" and 1½" squares.

2. Layer a marked 3½" square on one end of a blue piece, right sides together and making sure the marked line is oriented as shown. Sew on the marked line. Trim the excess corner fabric, ¼" from the stitched line. Make four units measuring 3½" × 6½", including seam allowances. In the same way, make four reversed units, making sure to position the line in the opposite direction.

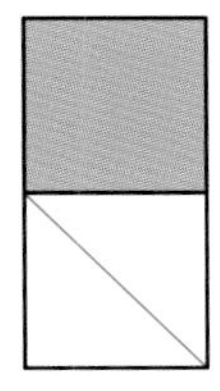
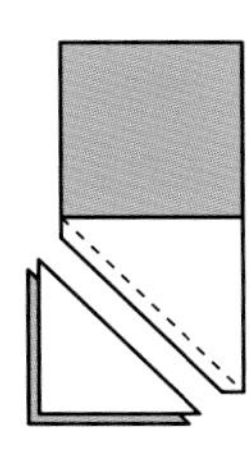
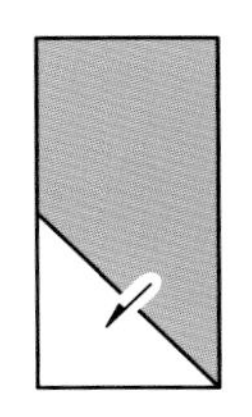
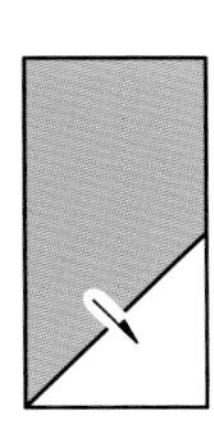

Make 4 of each unit, 3½" × 6½".

3. Layer marked 1½" squares on the upper-right and upper-left corners of a unit from step 2, right sides together. Sew on the marked line. Trim the excess corner fabric, ¼" from the stitched line. Make four units and four reversed units measuring 3½" × 6½", including seam allowances.

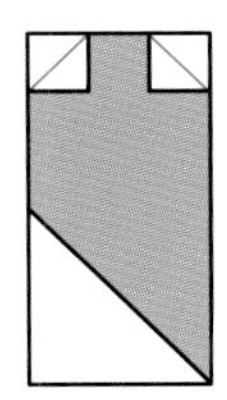
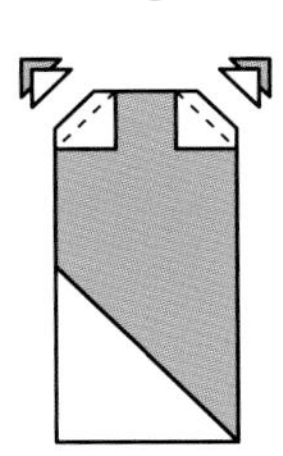
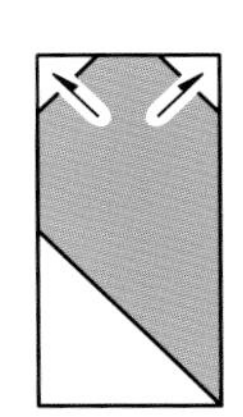
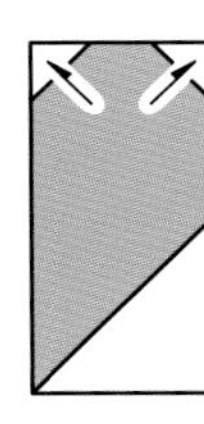

Make 4 of each unit, 3½" × 6½".

4. Join a unit and a reversed unit from the same print to make a Heart block. Make four blocks measuring 6½" square, including seam allowances.

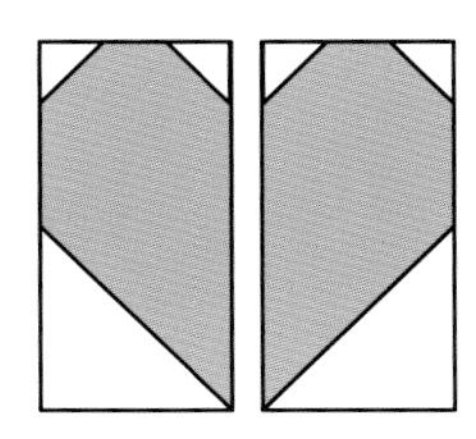
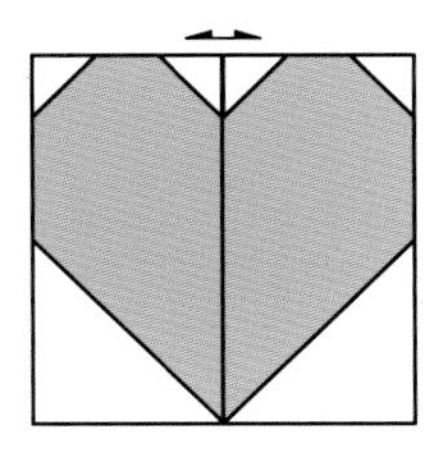

Make 4 blocks, 6½" × 6½".

Making the Sashing Units

1. Draw a diagonal line from corner to corner on the wrong side of the white 3" squares. Layer a marked square on a pink stripe square, right sides together. Sew ¼" from both sides of the drawn line. Cut the unit apart on the marked line to make two half-square-triangle units. Trim the units to measure 2½" square, including seam allowances. Make 12 pink units.

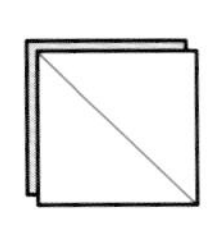
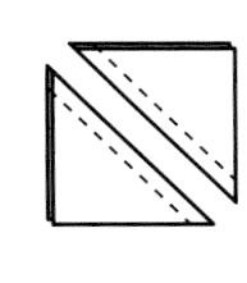
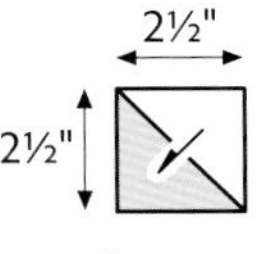

Make 12 units.

2. Repeat step 1 using the remaining marked white squares and the green squares to make 36 green units measuring 2½" square, including seam allowances.

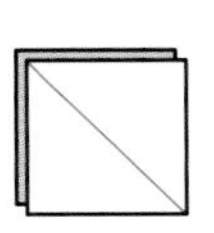
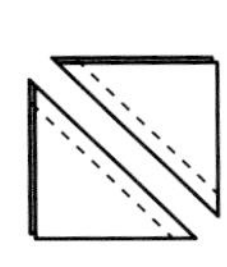
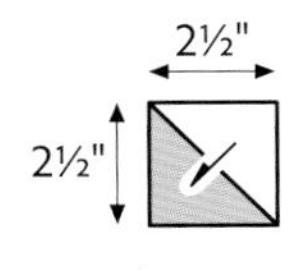

Make 36 units.

3. Lay out two green units, two pink units, and two white 2½" squares in two rows of three as shown on page 56, noting the orientation of the units. Sew the units and squares into rows. Join the rows to make a

sashing unit measuring 4½" × 6½", including seam allowances. Make four units. The remaining green units will be used for the pieced border.

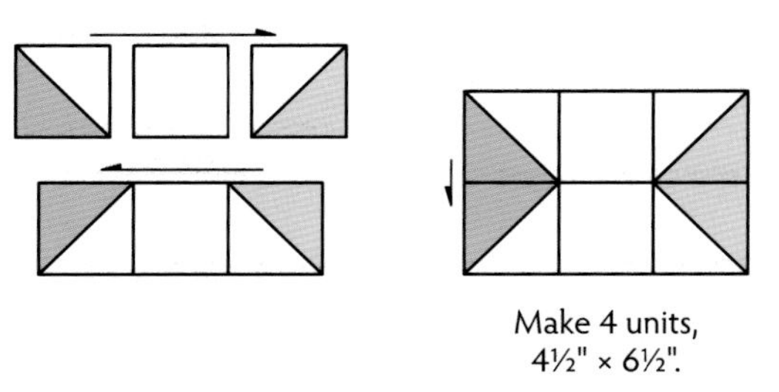

Make 4 units,
4½" × 6½".

4. Join four pink units to make a center unit, noting the orientation of the units. Make one unit measuring 4½" square, including seam allowances.

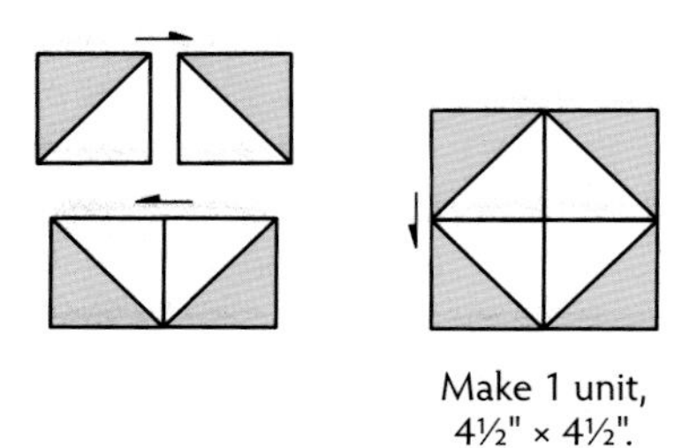

Make 1 unit,
4½" × 4½".

Assembling the Quilt Top

1. Lay out the blocks, sashing units, and center unit in three rows, rotating the sashing units to form a pink diamond in the center. Sew the blocks and units into rows. Join the rows to make a quilt-top center that measures 16½" square, including seam allowances.

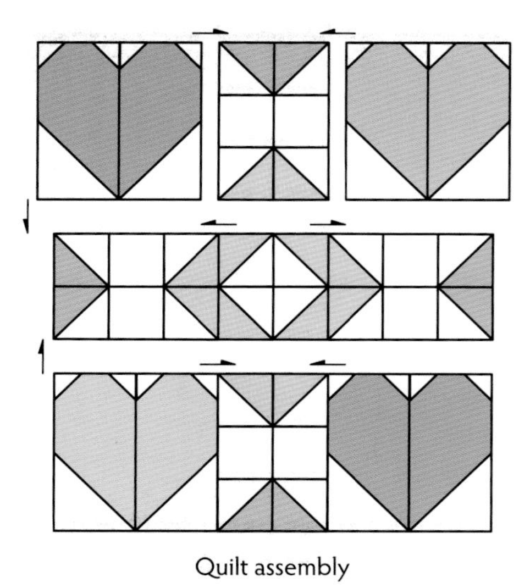

Quilt assembly

2. Join six green half-square-triangle units and two white 2½" squares, rotating units as shown, to make a side border measuring 2½" × 16½", including seam allowances. Make two. Make top and bottom borders in the same way, adding a green triangle unit to each end. The top and bottom borders should be 2½" × 20½", including seam allowances.

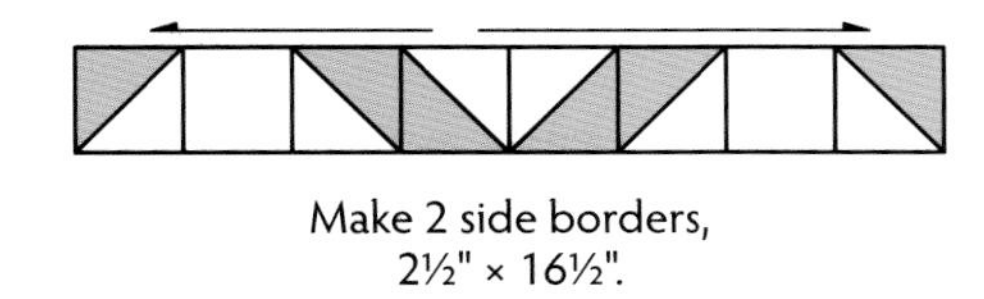

Make 2 side borders, 2½" × 16½".

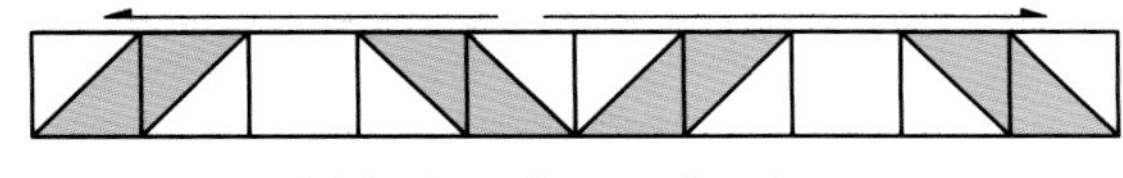

Make 2 top/bottom borders, 2½" × 20½".

3. Sew the borders to the sides first, and then the top and bottom edges. The quilt top should measure 20½" square, including seam allowances.

4. Sew the white 1½" × 20½" strips to opposite sides of the quilt top. Sew the white 1½" × 22½" strips to the top and bottom. The quilt top should measure 2½" × 22½", including seam allowances.

5. Sew the cream 3" × 22½" strips to opposite sides of the quilt top. Sew the cream 3" × 27½" strips to the top and bottom. The quilt top should measure 27½" square.

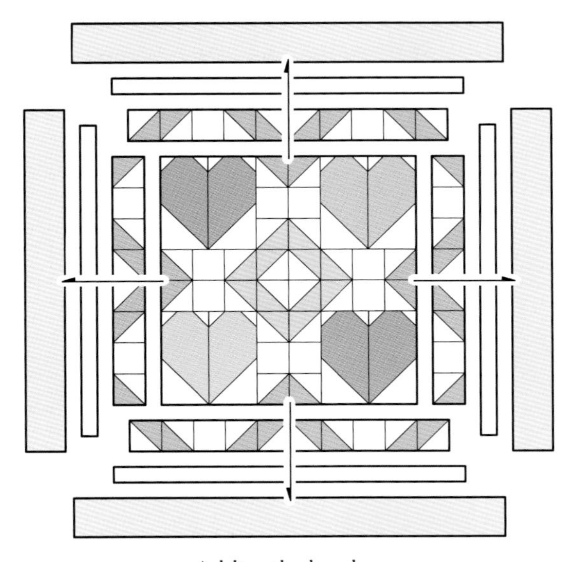

Adding the borders

Finishing the Quilt

For more details on any finishing steps, visit ShopMartingale.com/HowtoQuilt for free downloadable information.

1. Layer the quilt top with batting and backing; baste the layers together.

2. Quilt by hand or machine. The quilt shown is machine quilted with an allover swirl pattern.

3. Use the pink print 2¼"-wide strips to make binding and then attach the binding to the quilt.

ADD A ROD POCKET

I always make a rod pocket when I think that I might want to hang a quilt on a wall. If I end up using the quilt as a table topper, the rod pocket doesn't interfere, and I can use the quilt interchangeably.

To make a rod pocket for a quilt, cut a strip of fabric that's 4" wide and 2" shorter than the width of the quilt (for this quilt, the strip would be 4" × 25½"). Fold the ends under ½", and then ½" again to make a hem. Stitch in place. Fold the strip in half, wrong sides together. Baste the raw edges to the top of the quilt back. The top edge of the rod pocket will be secured when the binding is sewn on the quilt. Finish the rod pocket after the binding has been attached by hand stitching the folded edge to the back of the quilt. Insert a dowel, and the project is ready to hang on the wall.

Hearts at Home Runner

PIECED BY SHERRI McCONNELL; QUILTED BY MARION BOTT

After making the Hearts at Home Quilt (page 53), I decided that the block design would make a fun runner. The chain-link design creates an interesting impact whether pieced with one fabric or with several different colors as shown. I used the Canning Day collection by Corey Yoder for this cheerful runner.

FINISHED RUNNER: 57½" × 17½"
FINISHED BLOCK: 10" × 10"

Materials

Yardage is based on 42"-wide fabric. Fat eighths measure 9" × 21".

- ⅞ yard of white solid for blocks and inner border
- 10 fat eighths of assorted prints (2 green, 2 coral, 2 pink, 2 aqua, and 2 yellow) for blocks and binding
- ⅜ yard of green print for outer border
- 1⅜ yards of fabric for backing
- 24" × 64" piece of batting

Cutting

All measurements include ¼"-wide seam allowances.

From the white solid, cut:
1 strip, 3½" × 42"; crosscut into 10 squares, 3½" × 3½"
3 strips, 3" × 42"; crosscut into 30 squares, 3" × 3"
2 strips, 2½" × 42"; crosscut into 20 squares, 2½" × 2½"
5 strips, 1½" × 42"; crosscut *2 of the strips* into:
 2 strips, 1½" × 12½"
 20 squares, 1½" × 1½"

From *each* of 1 green, 1 coral, 1 pink, 1 aqua, and 1 yellow print, cut:
2 pieces, 3½" × 6½" (10 total)
1 strip, 2¼" × 21"; crosscut into 2 strips, 2¼" × 9" (10 total)

From *each* of 1 green, 1 coral, 1 pink, 1 aqua, and 1 yellow print, cut:
6 squares, 3" × 3" (30 total)
1 strip, 2¼" × 21"; crosscut into 2 strips, 2¼" × 9" (10 total)

From the green print, cut:
4 strips, 3" × 42"; crosscut *1 of the strips* into 2 strips, 3" × 17½"

Making the Blocks

Press seam allowances in the directions indicated by the arrows.

1. Draw a diagonal line from corner to corner on the wrong side of the white 3½" and 1½" squares.

2. Layer a marked 3½" square on one end of a green piece, right sides together and making sure the marked line is oriented as shown. Sew on the marked line. Trim the excess corner fabric, ¼" from the stitched line. Make five units, one of each color, measuring 3½" × 6½", including seam allowances. In the same way, make five reversed units, one of each color, making sure to position the line in the opposite direction.

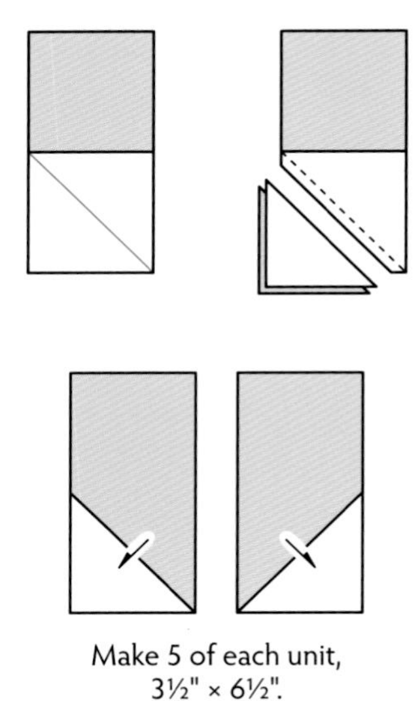

Make 5 of each unit,
3½" × 6½".

3. Layer marked 1½" squares on the upper-right and upper-left corners of a unit from step 2, right sides together. Sew on the marked line. Trim the excess corner fabric, ¼" from the stitched line. Make five units and five reversed units measuring 3½" × 6½", including seam allowances.

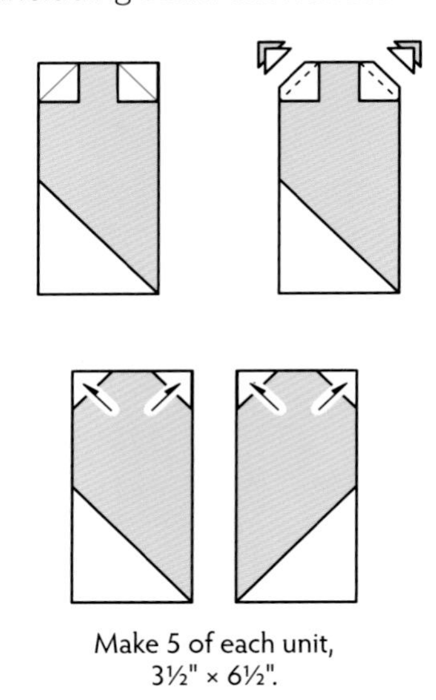

Make 5 of each unit,
3½" × 6½".

4. Join a unit and a reversed unit from the same print to make a heart unit. Make five units measuring 6½" square, including seam allowances.

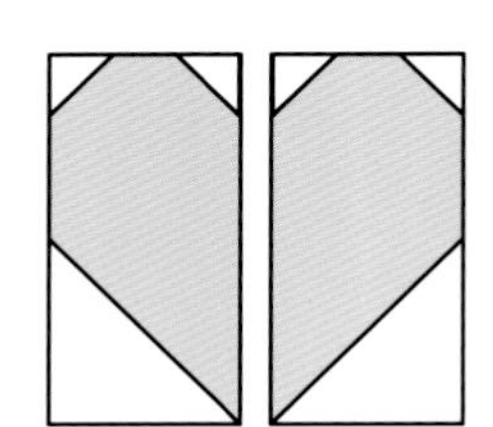

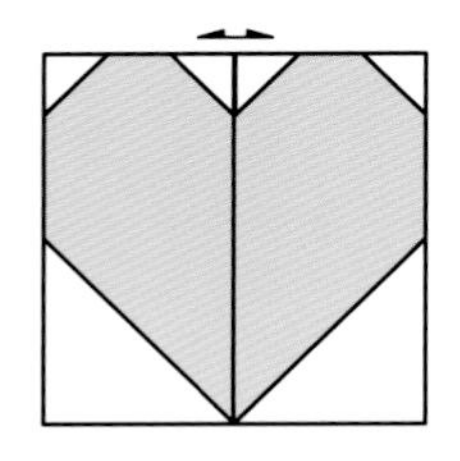

Make 5 units,
6½" × 6½".

5. Draw a diagonal line from corner to corner on the wrong side of the white 3" squares. Layer a marked square on a green 3" square, right sides together. Sew ¼" from both sides of the drawn line. Cut the unit apart on the marked line to make two half-square-triangle units. Trim the units to measure 2½" square, including seam allowances. Use all the colors of 3" squares to make five sets of 12 matching units (60 total).

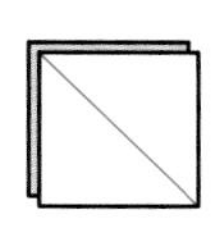

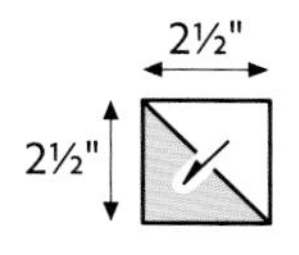

Make 5 sets of
12 matching units.

6. Join two matching half-square-triangle units and one white 2½" square to make a side row measuring 2½" × 6½", including seam allowances. Make five sets of two matching side rows. Then join four matching half-square-triangle units and one white 2½" square to make a top row measuring 2½" × 10½", including seam allowances. Repeat to make a bottom row. Make five sets of two matching top and bottom rows.

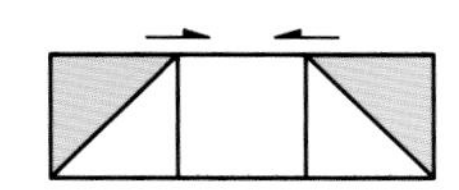

Make 5 sets of 2 matching side rows,
2½" × 6½".

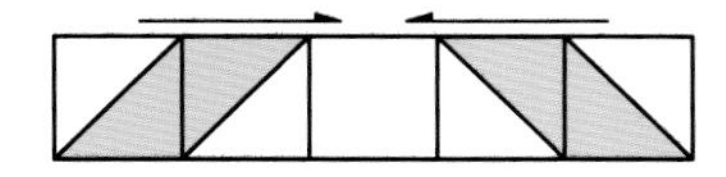

Make 5 sets of 2 matching top/bottom rows,
2½" × 10½".

7. Sew matching side rows to opposite sides of a heart unit. The triangle units and heart unit should be from the same color family. Sew matching top and bottom rows to the heart unit to make a block. Make five blocks measuring 10½" square, including seam allowances.

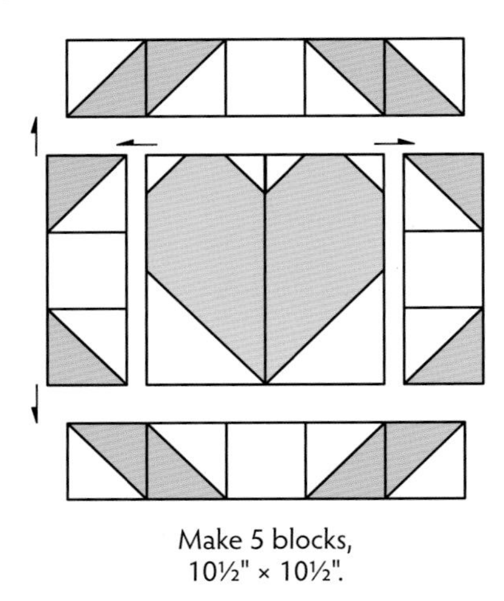

Make 5 blocks,
10½" × 10½".

Assembling the Runner

1. Join the blocks to make a row as shown in the table-runner assembly diagram below. The runner center should measure 50½" × 10½", including seam allowances.

2. Join the remaining white 1½"-wide strips end to end. From the pieced strip, cut two 50½"-long strips. Sew the strips to the long sides of the table runner. Sew the white 1½" × 12½" strips to the short ends of the runner. The runner should measure 52½" × 12½", including seam allowances.

3. Join the remaining green print 3" × 42" strips end to end. From the pieced strip, cut two 52½"-long strips. Sew the strips to the long sides of the table runner. Sew the green 3" × 17½" strips to the short ends of the runner, which should measure 57½" × 17½".

Finishing the Runner

For more details on any finishing steps, visit ShopMartingale.com/HowtoQuilt for free downloadable information.

1. Layer the runner top with batting and backing; baste the layers together.

2. Quilt by hand or machine. The runner shown is machine quilted with an allover swirls design.

3. Use the print 2¼" × 9" strips to make a scrappy binding and then attach the binding to the runner.

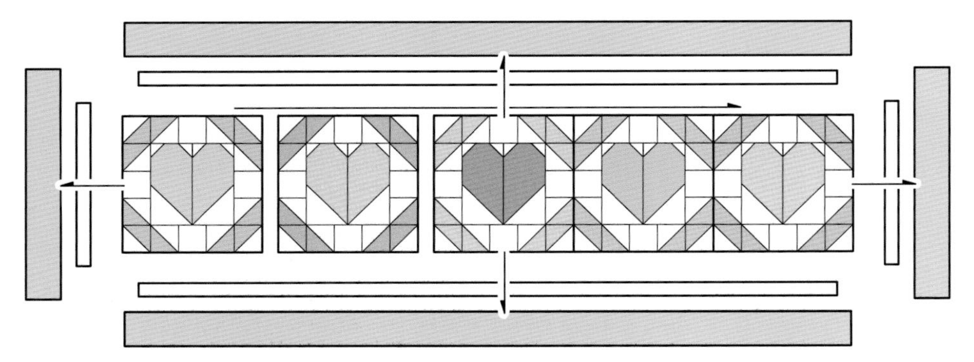

Table-runner assembly

Patchwork Project Bag

PIECED BY SHERRI McCONNELL; QUILTED BY MARION BOTT

Project bags tap into my penchant for organization, especially when I'm able to see what's inside. Use your bag to store your sewing supplies, or make one for a friend to store makeup or jewelry and other accessories.

FINISHED BAG: 10½" × 11½"

Materials

Yardage is based on 42"-wide fabric. Fat quarters measure 18" × 21".

* 5 squares, 2½" × 2½" *each,* of assorted prints for bag front
* ¼ yard of gray diagonal stripe for bag front and handle
* 1 square, 12" × 12", of gray print for bag back
* 1 square, 12" × 12", of yellow print for bag back
* 1 strip, 1" × 12", of pink print for zipper pull tab
* 1 fat quarter of pink stripe for bias binding
* ⅝ yard of white Shape Flex 20"-wide fusible interfacing for bag front and handle
* 1 rectangle, 5½" × 10½", of clear vinyl for bag front
* 12" × 12" square of Soft and Stable or batting
* 12" zipper
* ½" bias-tape maker

Cutting

All measurements include ¼"-wide seam allowances.

From the gray diagonal stripe, cut:
1 strip, 3" × 22"
1 strip, 3½" × 10½"
1 strip, 2½" × 10½"
1 strip, 1½" × 10½"

From the Shape Flex interfacing, cut:
1 strip, 3" × 22"
1 strip, 3½" × 10½"
1 strip, 2½" × 10½"

From the pink stripe, cut:
1 square, 18" × 18"

Making the Bag Front

Use a ¼" seam allowance. Press seam allowances in the directions indicated by the arrows.

1. Join the print 2½" squares to make a patchwork strip measuring 2½" × 10½.

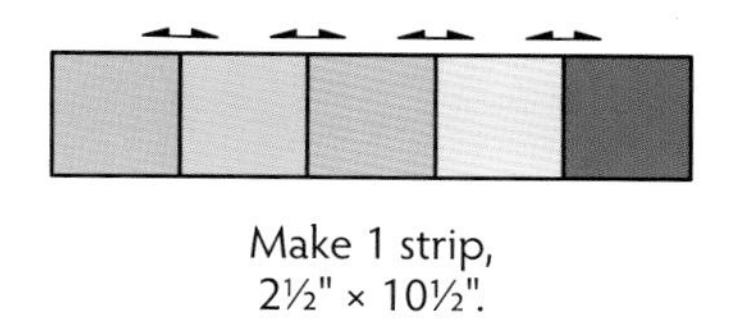

Make 1 strip,
2½" × 10½".

2. Sew the gray stripe 1½" × 10½" strip to the top edge of the patchwork strip to make a unit measuring 3½" × 10½", including seam allowances.

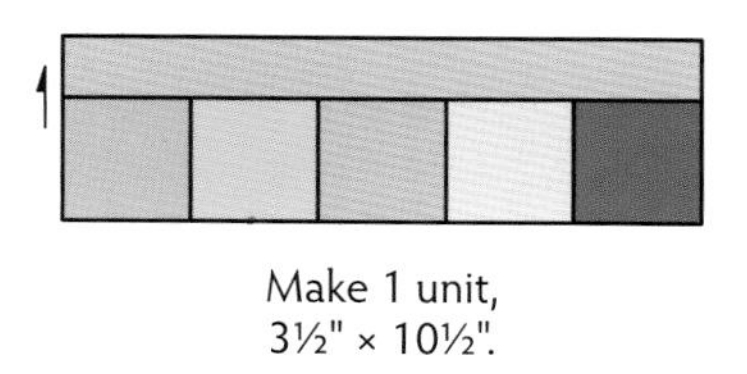

Make 1 unit,
3½" × 10½".

3. Fuse the interfacing 3½" × 10½" strip to the wrong side of the gray stripe 3½" × 10½" strip. Place the fused gray strip right side up on a flat surface. Place the vinyl rectangle on top of the gray strip and then place the unit from step 2 on top of the vinyl, *wrong* side up, aligning the raw edges. Stitch the layers together along their aligned edges. Turn right side out. Press, being careful not to touch the vinyl with the hot iron. Topstitch ¼" from the folded edge.

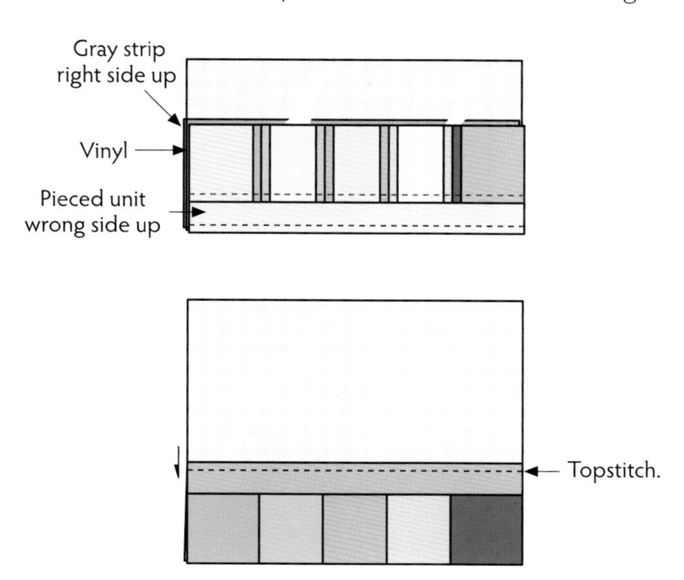

4. Fuse the interfacing 3" × 22" strip to the wrong side of the gray stripe 3" × 22" strip. Fold in half lengthwise. Press and cut into two pieces, 1½" × 11".

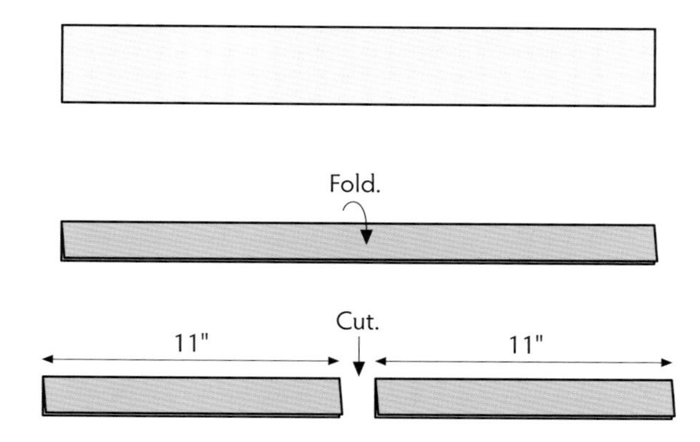

5. Unfold a gray strip from step 4 and place it on top of the zipper, right sides together. Sew on the creased line. Fold the gray strip in half again, wrong sides together. Press and topstitch ¼" from the folded edge. In the same way, sew the remaining gray strip to the other side of the zipper to make the zipper band. Trim the zipper band to measure 3½" × 10½", making sure the zipper pull is not extended beyond the ends of the fabric. Also, you don't want the zipper to come apart, so if you're trimming off the zipper stop, whipstitch by hand across the bottom end of the zipper to prevent unzipping too far.

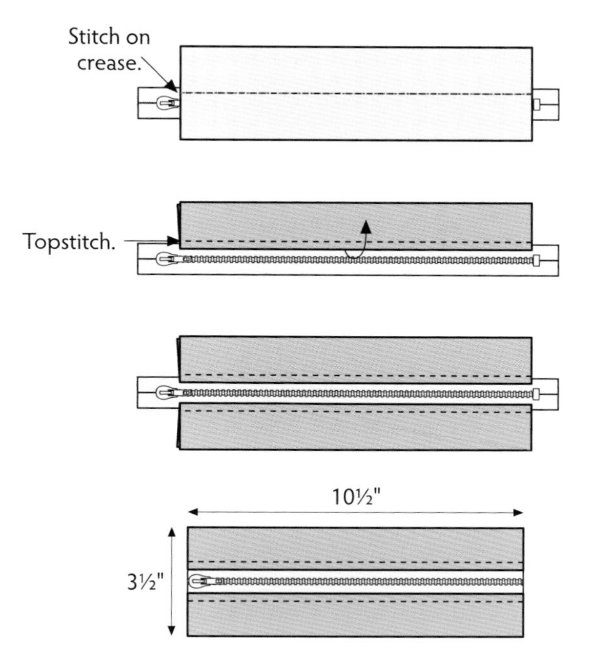

6. Place the zipper band, wrong side up, on top of the unit from step 3 and align the raw edges. Stitch the layers together. Press and then topstitch ¼" from the seamline. The bag front should measure 10½" × 11½", including seam allowances.

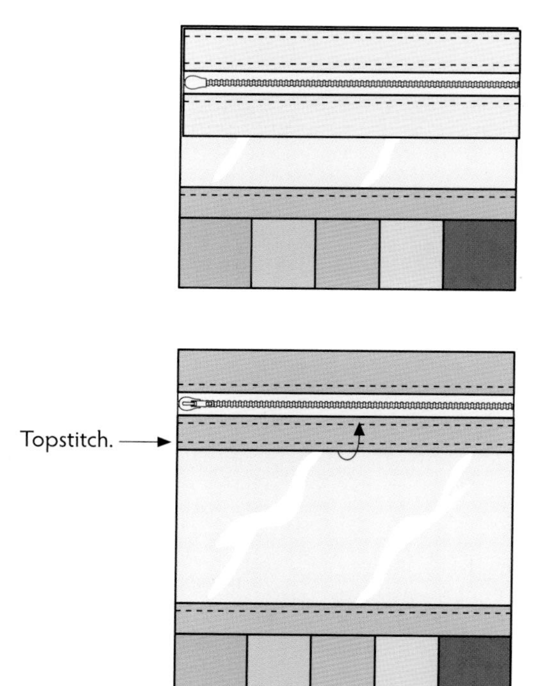

Make 1 bag front, 10½" × 11½".

Making the Bag Back

With wrong sides together, layer the gray print square, the Soft and Stable square, and the yellow square; baste together. Machine quilt with an allover feather plume design. Trim to 10½" × 11½".

BE PREPARED

I like to give my quilter Soft and Stable and the fabrics I plan to use and have her quilt an allover pattern. Then, when I'm ready to make a zipper bag or other project, I have my materials ready to go and the machine quilting is already done!

Finishing the Bag

1. On the bottom of the bag, use a pencil and a glass or small plate to mark a rounded corner so that the circle touches the sides of the bag. Repeat to mark both bottom corners on the bag front and back. Cut on the marked lines.

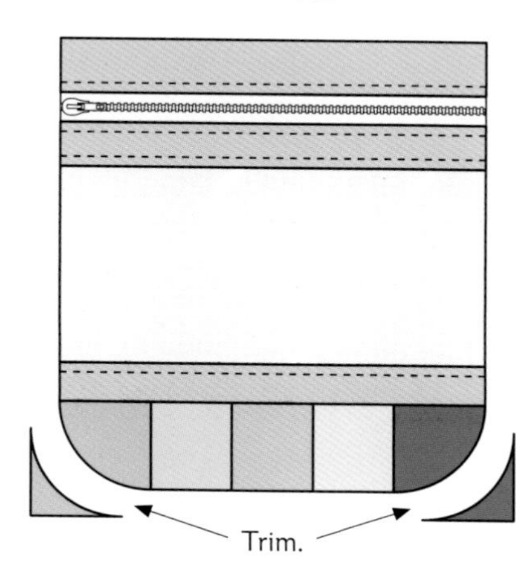

2. Fuse the interfacing 2½" × 10½" piece to the wrong side of the gray stripe 2½" × 10½" strip. Fold the strip in half lengthwise, right sides together, and sew along the long side to make a tube. Turn the tube right side out, center the seamline, and press. Make one handle measuring 1" × 10½", including seam allowances.

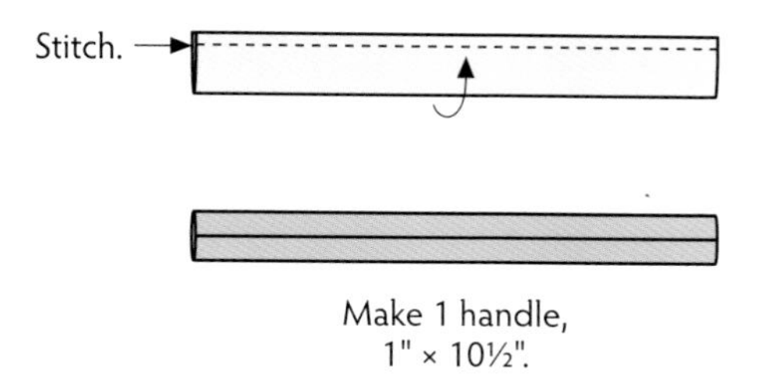

Make 1 handle,
1" × 10½".

3. On the bag back, mark 2" in from each side along the top edge. With the raw edges matching and the outer edges of the handle aligned with the 2" mark, baste the handle in place.

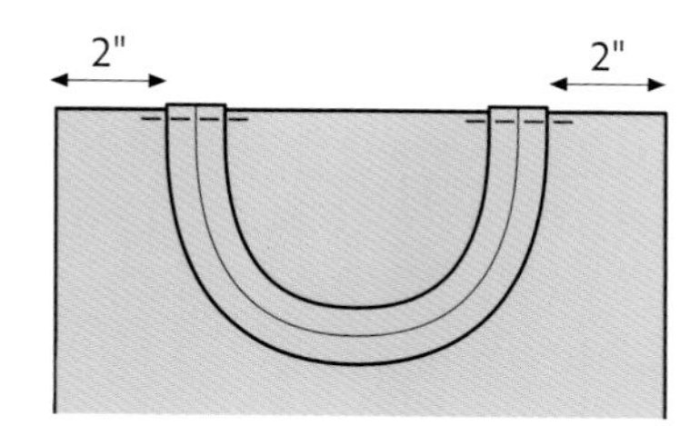

4. Layer the bag front and back, wrong sides together, and edgestitch around the perimeter using a ⅛" seam allowance.

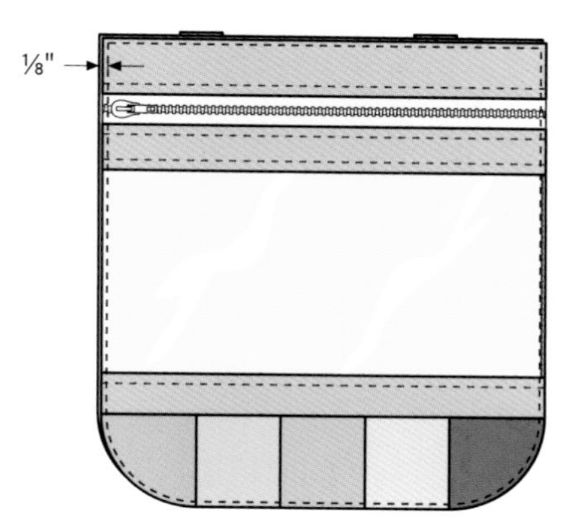

5. Referring to "Bias Binding" on page 77, use the pink stripe square to cut 2¼"-wide strips. Make 50" of bias binding. Attach the binding to the bag as you would a quilt.

6. To make a pull tab, insert one end of the pink print 1" × 12" strip into a ½" bias-tape maker. Pull the tip of the strip through the maker and then pull the bias-tape maker slowly along the strip, following close behind it with your iron to crease the edges of the fabric as it emerges from the bias-tape maker.

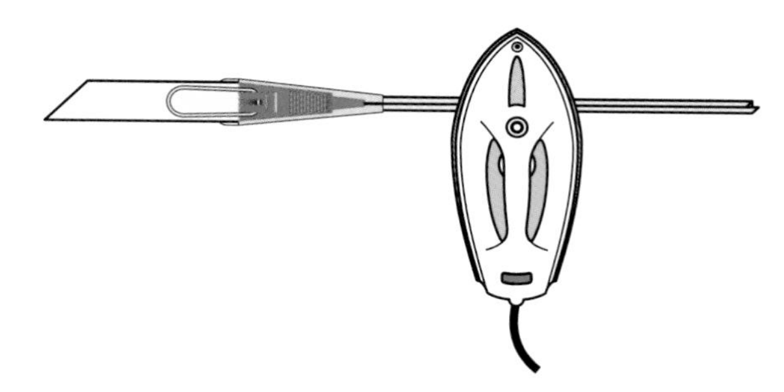

7. Fold the pink strip in half lengthwise and stitch along the open edge. Thread both ends of the pull tab through the zipper pull; slip the ends under the center of the strip and pull to secure. (See the photo at the top of page 66).

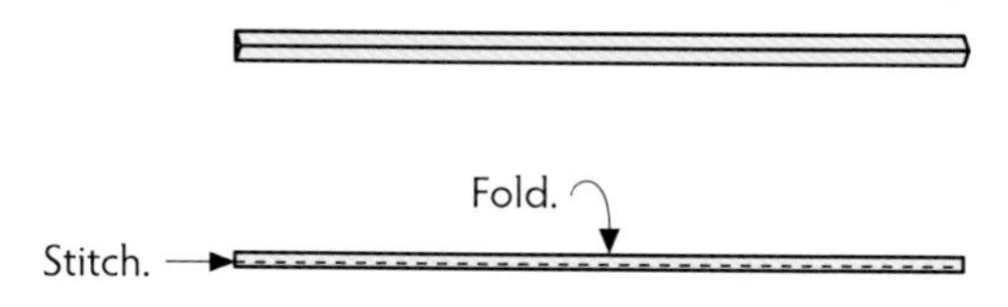

grid
OLFA
ROTARY CUTTER

Practically Perfect Storage

PIECED BY SHERRI McCONNELL; QUILTED BY MARION BOTT

Keep your favorite sewing tools at hand and in style with a pair of keepers. The rotary-cutter case protects the blade (and you) as you pack it in your bag. And the hexagon needle keeper is a quick-to-make cutie that can't be beat!

FINISHED CASE: 5" × 9"

Materials

Fat quarters measure 18" × 21".

- 1 piece, 6" × 10", of gray print for case front
- 1 piece, 6" × 10", of yellow floral for case back
- 1 piece, 6" × 8", of aqua print for pocket
- 1 piece, 6" × 8", of coordinating fabric for pocket lining
- 1 fat quarter of yellow print for binding
- ¼ yard of Soft and Stable

Cutting

All measurements include ¼"-wide seam allowances.

From the yellow print, cut:
1 square, 10" × 10"
1 strip, 2" × 5"

From the Soft and Stable, cut:
1 piece, 6" × 10"
1 piece, 6" × 8"

Assembling the Case

For more details on any of the steps below, visit ShopMartingale.com/HowtoQuilt for free downloadable information.

1. With wrong sides together, layer the gray, the Soft and Stable, and the yellow floral 6" × 10" pieces; baste the layers together. Machine quilt with an allover feather plume design. Trim the case front to measure 5" × 9", including seam allowances.

2. With wrong sides together, layer the aqua piece, the Soft and Stable 6" × 8" piece, and the lining piece; baste the layers together. Machine quilt with an allover swirl design. Trim the pocket to measure 5" × 7", including seam allowances.

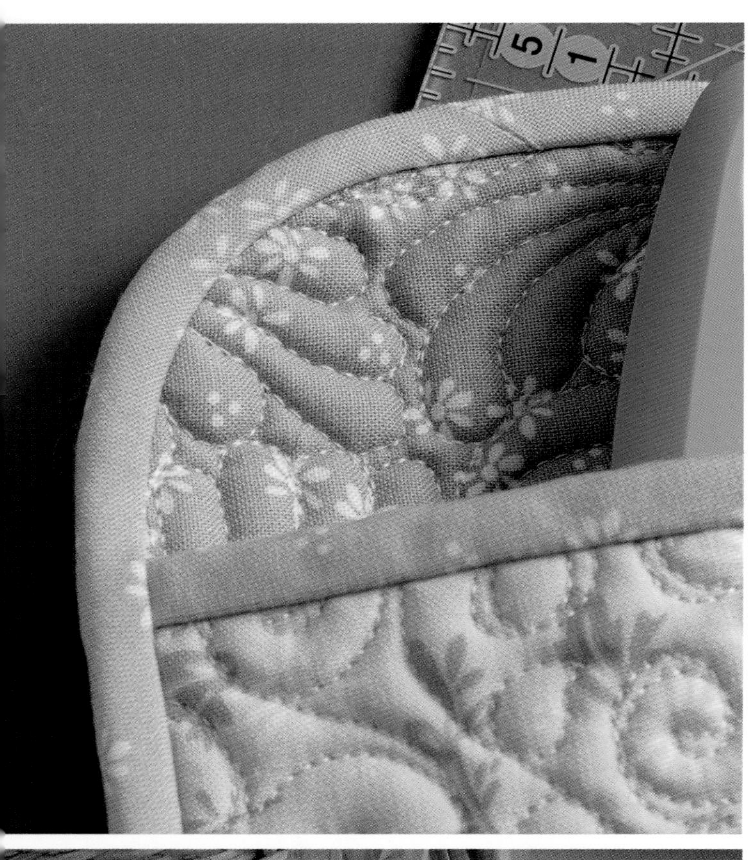

3. Bind one short end of the pocket as you would a quilt, using the yellow 2" × 5" strip.

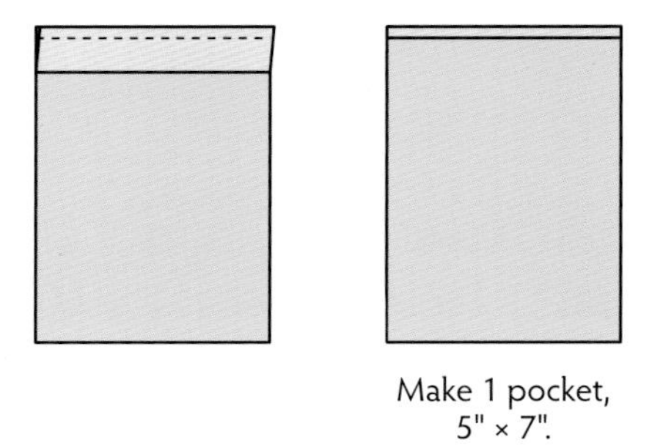

4. Use a pencil and a glass or small plate to mark rounded corners so that the circle touches the sides of the case. Mark all four corners on the case front and the bottom corners on the pocket. Cut on the marked lines.

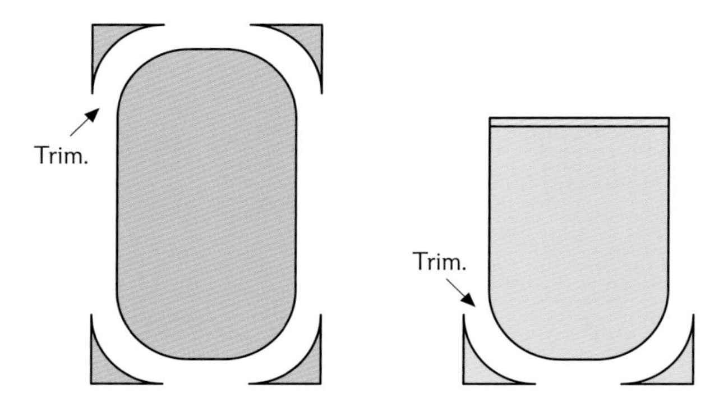

5. Place the pocket on top of the case front and edgestitch around the perimeter, ⅛" from the edges.

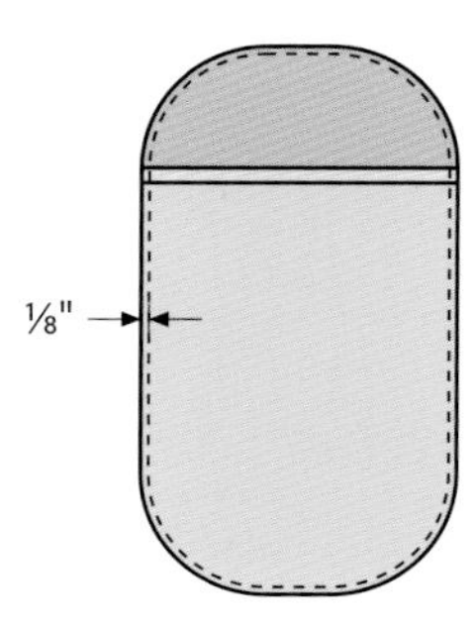

6. Referring to "Bias Binding" on page 77, use the yellow 10" square to cut 2"-wide strips. Make 40" of bias binding. Attach the binding to the case as you would a quilt.

Hexagon Needle Keeper

FINISHED NEEDLE KEEPER: 3¼" × 4½" (closed); 4½" × 6½" (open)

Materials

- 17 squares, 2½" × 3", of assorted prints for hexagons
- 1 piece, 5" × 7", of yellow floral for lining
- 1 piece, 5" × 5½", of white floral for pocket
- 1 piece, 3½" × 6", of beige wool or felt for needle page
- 6½" × 8" piece of batting
- 3" length of ¼"-wide elastic
- 1 button, ½" diameter
- Cardstock or other sturdy paper for hexagon foundations *OR* 1" precut hexagon paper pieces*
- Template plastic (optional)
- Paper punch (optional)
- Pinking shears

**PaperPieces.com is a good source for precut hexagons if you can't find them at your local quilt shop.*

Making the Hexagon Exterior

Skip steps 1 and 2 below if you have purchased precut foundation papers for 1" hexagons.

1. Trace the pattern on page 73 onto cardstock or template plastic. Cut it out just inside the traced lines to make a master template.

2. Trace the master template onto cardstock or sturdy paper 17 times. Cut out the paper hexagons just inside the traced lines. Be as accurate as possible when tracing and cutting so that all the shapes are exactly the same. Use a small paper punch (or scissors) to punch a hole in the center of each paper foundation.

3. Center a paper hexagon template on the wrong side of a print square. Pin through the center of the hole without piercing the template. Use the template as a guide to cut out a fabric hexagon about ⅜" larger than the template on all sides. Prepare 17 hexagons.

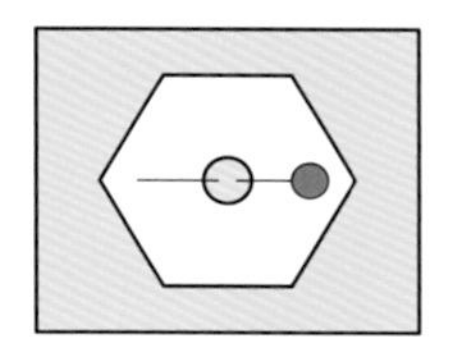

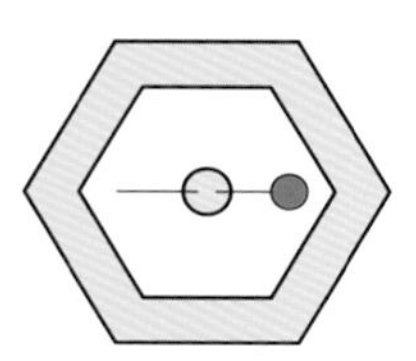

Make 17 hexagons.

MAKE IT EASIER

Instead of a ¼" seam allowance, I prefer to cut a ⅜"-wide seam allowance on all sides of the hexagon template to make basting easier. You don't need an exact seam allowance, because the paper foundation will provide a precise shape. Punching a hole in the center of each template makes removing the paper easier than if you baste or glue the template in place.

4. Fold the seam allowance over the template. Using regular sewing thread, stitch through the folded corners of the fabric to hold it securely in place around the paper. Don't stitch through the template. After the entire hexagon is basted, knot and clip the thread. Make 17 hexagons.

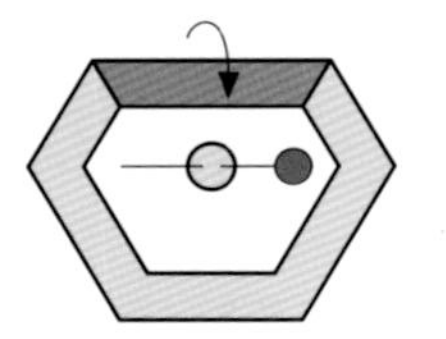

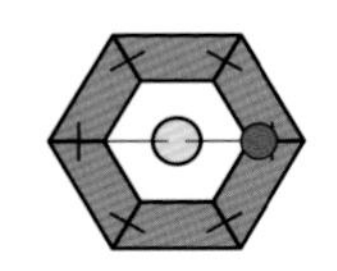

Make 17 hexagons.

5. Lay out the hexagons in five columns. Place the first two hexagons you want to join right sides together. With a single strand of thread, whipstitch them together from corner to corner, catching only the folded fabric edges. Repeat to join the hexagons into rows and then join the rows to make the hexagon exterior. Press and then remove the paper templates.

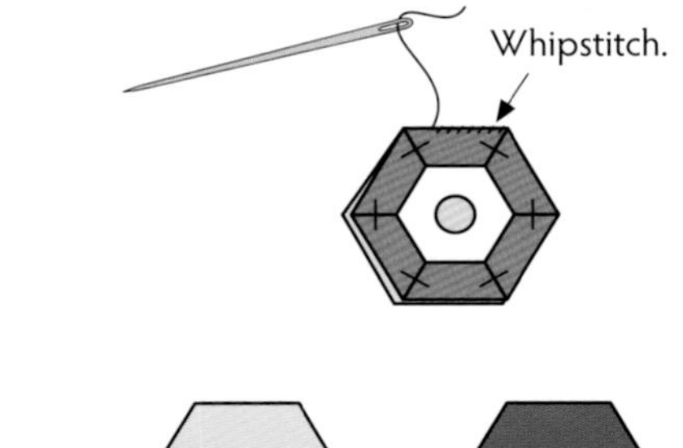

6. Trim the hexagon exterior to measure 5" × 7", including seam allowances. Machine baste ⅛" around the perimeter.

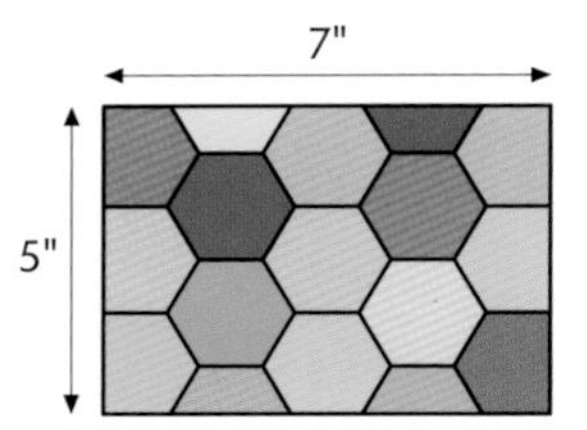

7. Layer the hexagon exterior with batting; baste the layers together. Hand or machine quilt. The needle keeper shown is hand quilted ¼" from the edges of some of the hexagons. After quilting, trim the batting even with the edges of the needle keeper exterior.

Assembling the Needle Keeper

1. To make the pocket, fold the white floral fabric in half, wrong sides together, to make a 2¾" × 5" pocket. Place the pocket on the right (front) side of the yellow floral piece, aligning the raw edges on the left. Baste the sides of the pocket ⅛" from the outer edges. Draw a line where you would like to divide the pocket, and then sew on the line, starting and stopping with a backstitch. I divided my pocket 1½" in from one side. This will be the lining.

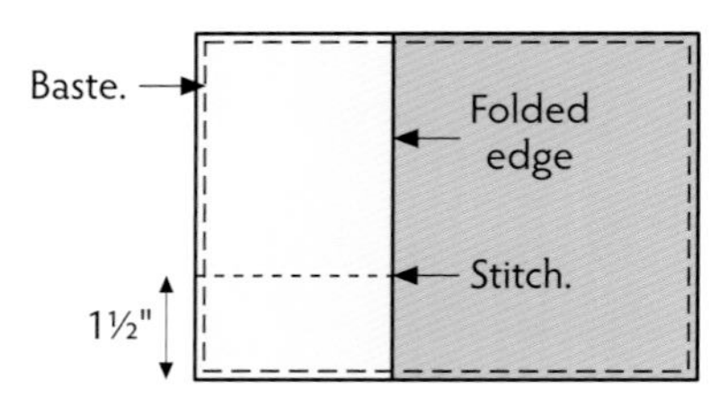

2. Fold the elastic in half and center the ends on one short end of the hexagon exterior as shown. Baste in place.

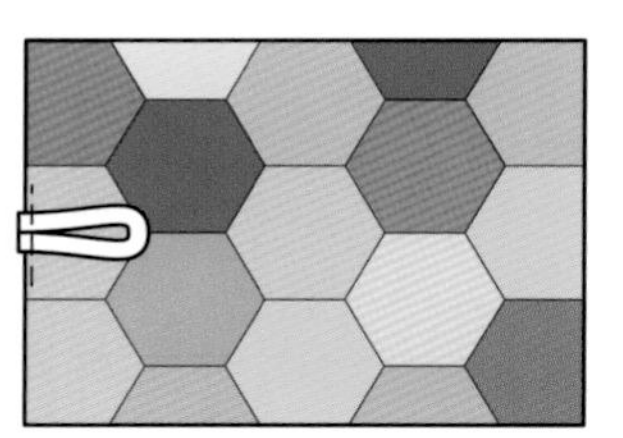

3. Place the hexagon exterior and the lining right sides together with the pocket on top of the elastic. Sew around the perimeter using a scant ¼" seam allowance and leaving a 2" opening for turning.

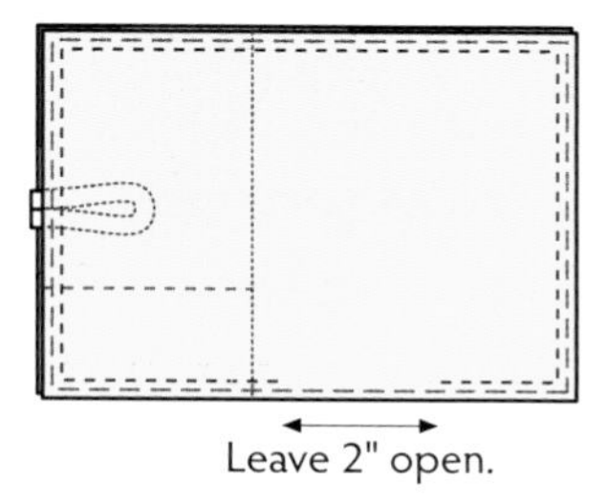

4. Turn the needle keeper right side out and press well. Slip-stitch the opening closed.

5. To add the needle page, fold the needle keeper in half and press. Unfold the needle keeper, lining side up. Fold the beige wool or felt piece in half. Place the wool or felt piece on top of the lining, matching center creases and centering the needle page from side to side. Sew on the center crease, starting and stopping with a backstitch. Use pinking shears to trim the ends of the needle page.

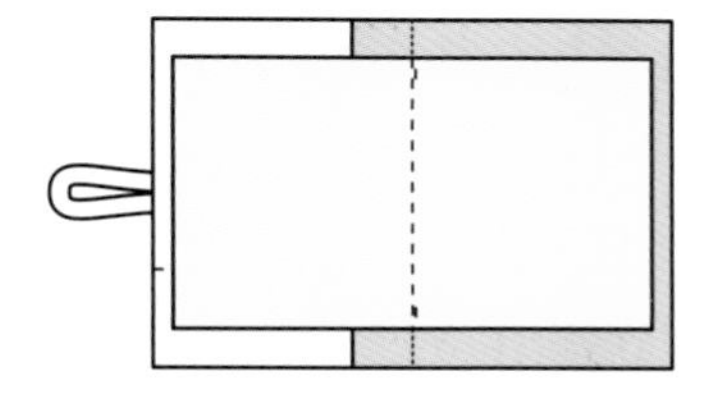

6. Attach the button to the front of the needle keeper.

MAKE IT YOUR OWN

You can add more than one wool or felt piece if you'd like more needle pages.

BUTTON OR RIBBON

I had a lot of fun choosing an old button from my great-grandmother's button collection, which was left in the drawer of her treadle sewing machine. I'll always think of her when I use this needle keeper. The keeper would be equally pretty with a piece of ribbon used to tie it closed.

If you'd prefer to use a ribbon, cut two 11"-long pieces of ¼"-wide ribbon. Center a piece of ribbon on each short end of the hexagon exterior before sewing the exterior and lining together, being careful not to catch the ribbons in any of the outer seams.

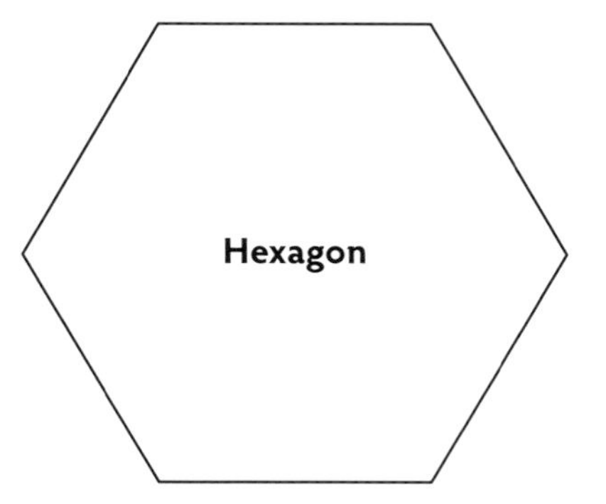

Finishing Basics

In this section, you'll find instructions for making pillow backs with a hidden zipper and my favorite method for making bias binding. For more details on other finishing techniques, find free downloadable information at ShopMartingale.com/HowtoQuilt.

Pillow Finishing

I finish nearly all of my pillows with a zippered back and sometimes quilt the pillow back because it gives the pillow extra body. The Mini Log Cabins Pillow (page 25) and Blooming Pillow (page 41) do not have quilted backs, but the back on the Garden Blooms Pillow (page 47) is quilted. Here are simple instructions to finish any pillow using my favorite techniques.

1. For the pillow back, cut a piece to the size indicated in the project instructions. Then cut one piece each of batting and muslin that are the same size as the pillow back.

2. If you want to quilt the pillow back, cut a piece that's 4" larger than the pillow top so that you have 2" on all sides. Layer the pillow back, batting, and muslin; baste the layers together. Hand or machine quilt. After quilting, cut the back into two pieces as instructed in the cutting instructions for the pillow you're making.

3. From a coordinating fabric, cut a 4"-wide strip as indicated in the project instructions. Do not quilt the strip. Press the strip in half lengthwise, *wrong* sides together. This will be the zipper flap.

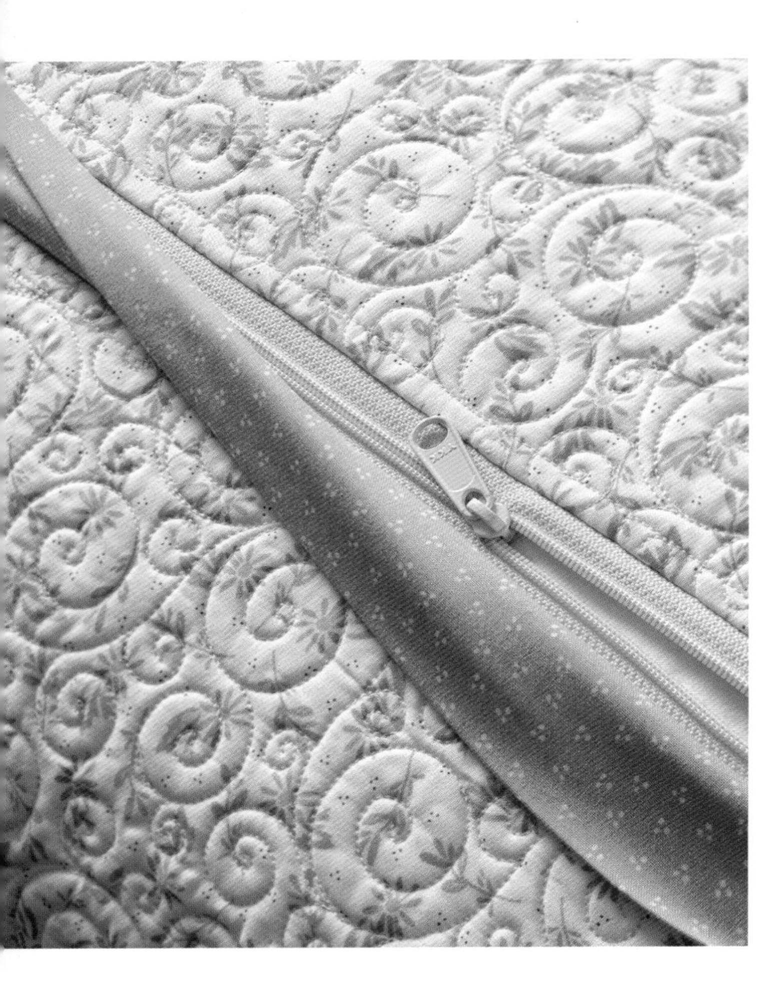

4. Align the flap right sides together with one raw edge of a pillow-back rectangle. Place the zipper along the raw edges, right side down. The zipper edge should align with the raw edges of the flap and pillow back. Any extra zipper length should extend beyond the fabric. It'll be trimmed later. Use a zipper foot to sew the zipper using a ¼" seam allowance.

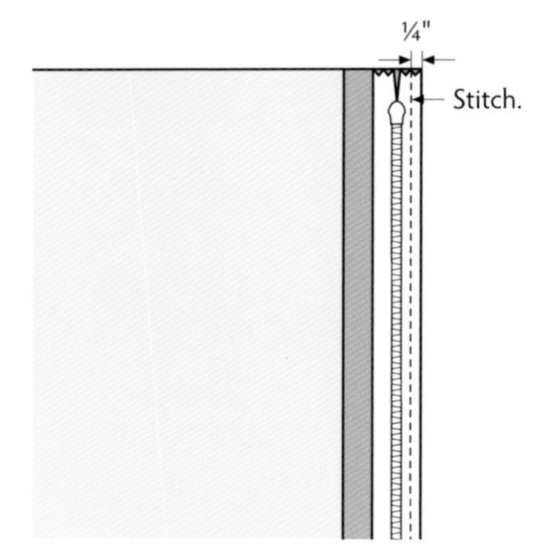

5. Place the second pillow-back piece right sides together with the unsewn side of the zipper, aligning the zipper edge with the raw edge of the pillow back. Pin or use binding clips to secure the zipper and then sew in place using a ¼" seam allowance.

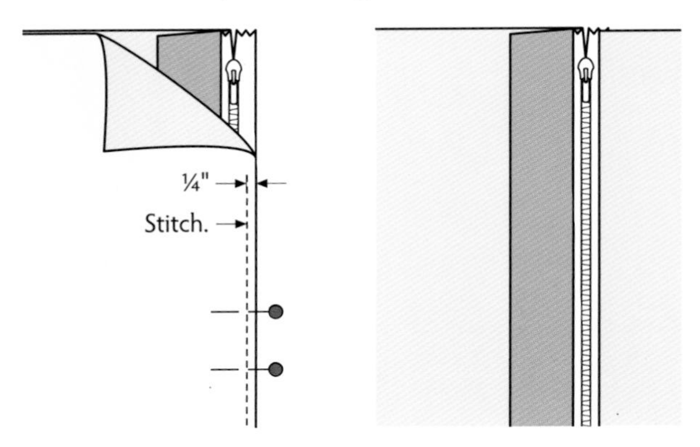

6. Press the flap so that it covers the zipper; topstitch ¼" from the flap seam.

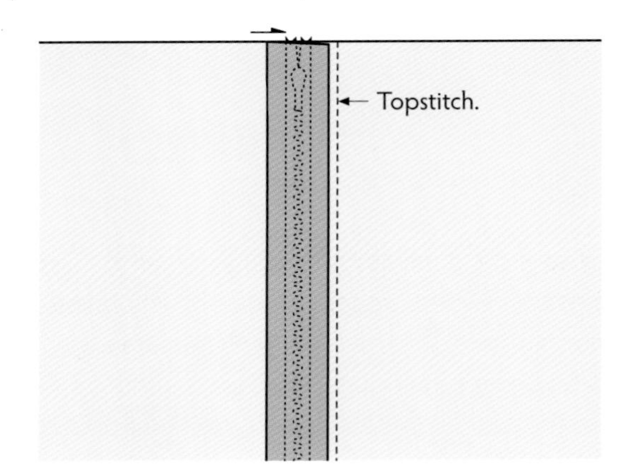

7. Centering the zipper, place the pillow front on the pillow back, wrong sides together. Unzip the zipper halfway. Pin (or use clips) and sew around the edges using a ¼" seam allowance.

8. Trim any excess length from the end of the zipper. Trim the pillow back even with the pillow top if needed.

9. Following the project instructions for the pillow you're making, prepare double-fold binding and use it to bind the outer edges of the pillow.

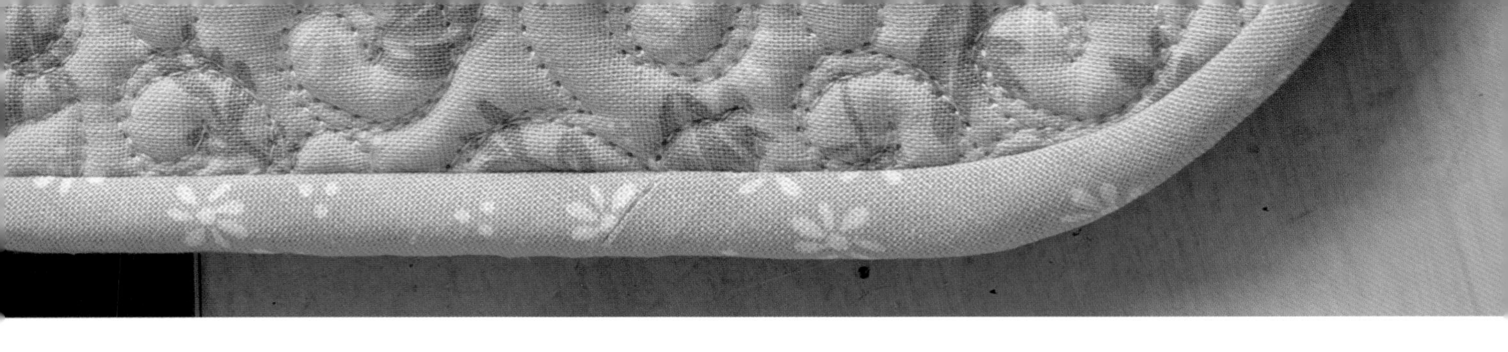

Bias Binding

When a project has round corners, you need to use bias binding so that the binding will stretch around the curves. Here's my method for making bias binding.

1. Cut a square of fabric to the size indicated in the project instructions. Cut the square in half diagonally.

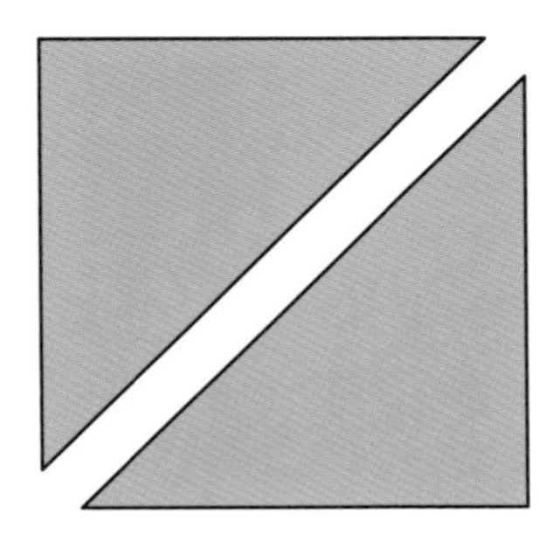

2. Sew the two halves back together along their short edges, as shown, to make a parallelogram. Notice that when aligning the triangles, the tip of one triangle should extend ¼" beyond the edge of the other triangle. Press the seam allowances open.

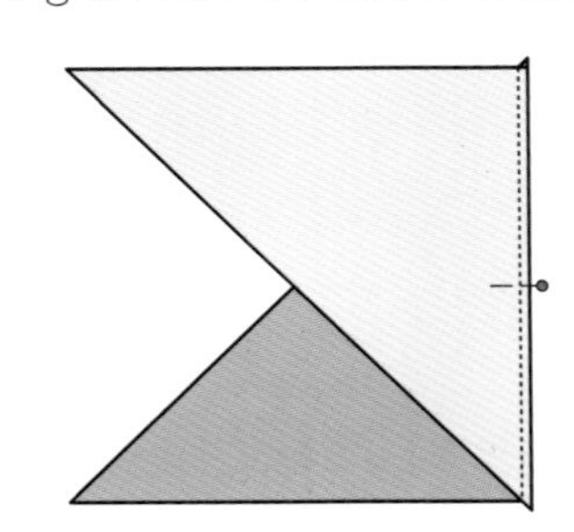

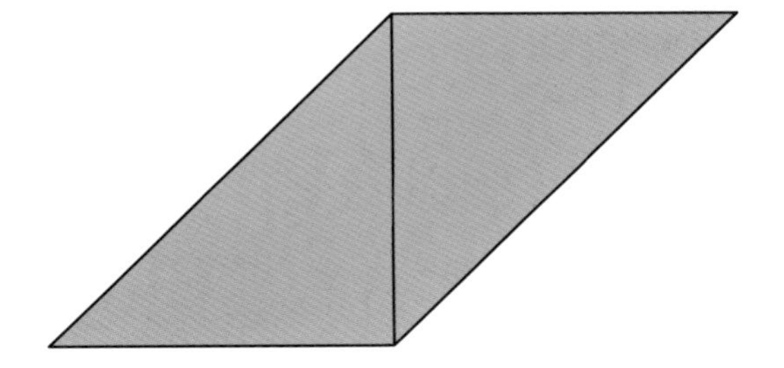

3. Using a ruler and rotary cutter, cut strips the width indicated in the project instructions. When you reach the end of the fabric, if you have any left over that would be narrower than the width of your binding strip, simply trim it off.

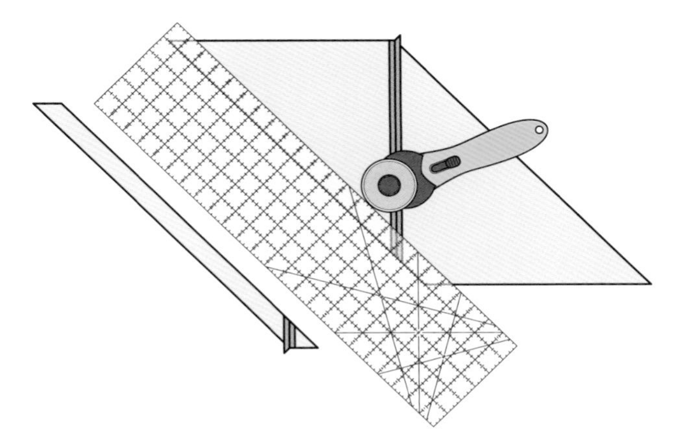

4. Using a ¼" seam allowance, sew the strips together end to end to make one long piece of binding. Press the seam allowances open and trim off the dog-ears.

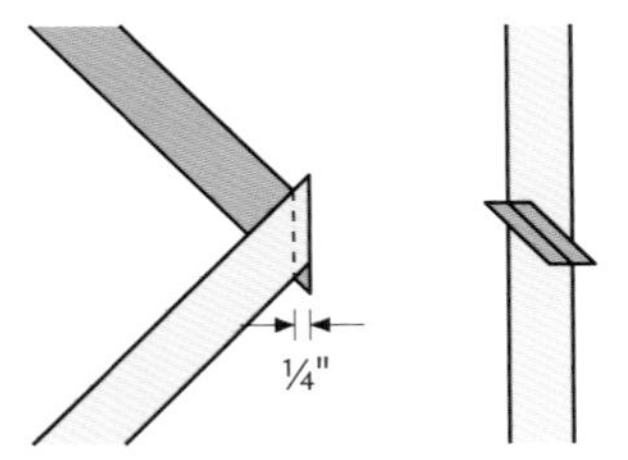

Press seam allowances open.

5. Carefully press the strip in half lengthwise; it will be stretchy since it's cut on the bias. Attach the binding as you would for straight-of-grain binding.

Decorating with Quilts, Pillows, and Runners

Begin by taking inventory of all of the quilts you have available to use for decor in your home. Note where and during what season you decorate with quilts and quilted items. Take notes of areas you need decor items. Measure those areas and come up with a list of projects to make. Decorate quarterly by changing the decor on the first day of March, June, September, and December. Below are a few ideas for decorating with quilts, pillows, and runners.

Quilts

* Use pianos and piano benches to display quilts.
* Drape quilts over couches, chairs, and ladders.
* Hang quilts on walls just as you would a painting.
* Place square quilts diagonally on a bed.

Pillows

* Place small pillows in a table-top basket or tray.
* Medium-sized pillows are perfect for displaying on children's rocking chairs.
* Prop up medium-sized pillows on shelves and display cases.
* Large pillows can be used as decor items in baskets and bins under tables or next to sofas.

Runners

* Use runners as dresser toppers—table runners aren't just for tables!
* Turn runners and toppers at an angle—not everything needs to be placed with straight lines.

Storing Quilts, Pillows, and Runners

Once you've made more than a few quilts, pillows, and runners, you'll undoubtedly need to store some while others are in use. Below are storage tips. Be sure to rotate quilted items that might be stored in plain sight. In most areas, I rotate them seasonally. In areas with more natural light, I rotate monthly. Even indirect sunlight can damage or fade fabrics.

Quilts

* If you have a spare bedroom or bed, lay out quilts flat for wrinkle-free storage.
* Dedicate closet shelves to quilt storage. You might wish to redo shelves to make a nice width.
* Armoires and cabinets provide practical and decorative quilt storage.
* Bookshelves can also function as terrific storage space to store and display smaller quilts.

Pillows

Make a list of each decorative pillow, its size, and the place where you store it when it's not in use.

* Store pillows separately from pillow forms to save space. Pillow forms can be used throughout the year with different covers.
* Store pillows in baskets, on shelves, or in closets.
* You can also store pillows in trunks or drawers.

Runners

* Roll runners to prevent wrinkles and store easily.
* Turn runners into decor even when not in use by rolling up and displaying them in a basket.
* Store in drawers or trunks.

About the Author

I was not going to be a quilter. My grandmother was a quilter, and she cut up perfectly good fabrics just to sew them back together. She went to guild meetings and met with her smaller quilting groups to sew and exchange blocks. She wore quilt block T-shirts and went to quilt shows. She even entered quilt shows and won blue ribbons. She loved hand quilting in the evenings with her stand-up frame and her lap frame. She made quilts and wall hangings and place mats and table runners. And she gifted many lovely things to me and her other family members.

But because of her, and with her help, I made my very first quilt. Oh, how wise she was! I became a quilter almost overnight. I started making small projects that I hand quilted to give to family and friends. I bought quilt books and pored over the lovely pages for inspiration. Slowly, over the years, I found more and more time to sew. I also discovered the wide world of quilting blogs with inspiration at my fingertips. I bought fabric. I made quilts of all sizes. I started buying quilting T-shirts. I sewed late into the evenings when my children were asleep and my husband was at work. And I met the most wonderful and amazing people who love quilting as I do, as my grandmother did, and her grandmothers before her.

I am a quilter! I'm ever thankful for the love of my family members who have always encouraged and supported me in every aspect of life, including quilting. And I'm also ever thankful for the quilting community that I know online and in real life. Your encouragement and support and inspiration mean the world to me. Happy quilting!